D1495583

HELPING THE NONCOMPLIANT CHILD

HELPING THE NONCOMPLIANT CHILD

A Clinician's Guide to Parent Training

REX L. FOREHAND
University of Georgia

ROBERT J. MCMAHON
University of British Columbia

Foreword by Robert G. Wahler

THE GUILFORD PRESS
New York   London

Printed in the United States of America
Last digit is print number 9 8 7 6 5 4

Library of Congress Cataloging in Publication Data

Forehand, Rex L. (Rex Lloyd), 1945–
  Helping the noncompliant child.

  Bibliography: p.
  Includes index.
  1. Family psychotherapy.   2. Children—Management.
I. McMahon, Robert J. (Robert Joseph), 1953–
II. Title.   [DNLM: 1. Child behavior disorders—Therapy.
2. Parent-child relations.   3. Parents—Psychology.
WS 350.6 F714h]
RC488.5.F67   649′.64   81-6629
ISBN 0-89862-611-0   AACR2

ACKNOWLEDGMENTS

Appreciation is expressed to the following presses/publishers for granting us permission to reproduce portions of our previously published material.

1. ACADEMIC PRESS
   Forehand, R. Child noncompliance to parental requests: Behavioral analysis and treatment. In M. Hersen, R. M. Eisler, & P. M. Miller (Eds.), *Progress in behavior modification* (Vol. 5). New York: Academic Press, 1977.
2. BRUNNER/MAZEL PUBLISHERS
   McMahon, R. J., Forehand, R., & Griest, D. L. Parent behavioral training to modify child noncompliance: Factors in generalization and maintenance. In R. B. Stuart & P. O. Davidson (Eds.), *Behavioral medicine: Therapeutic compliance, generalization, and maintenance.* New York: Brunner/Mazel, in press.
3. THE GUILFORD PRESS
   Atkeson, B. M., & Forehand, R. Conduct disorders. In E. J. Mash & L. G. Terdal (Eds.), *Behavioral assessment of childhood disorders.* New York: Guilford Press, 1981.
4. JOHN WILEY & SONS, INC.
   Wells, K. C., & Forehand, R. Childhood behavior problems in the home. In S. M. Turner, K. S. Calhoun, & H. E. Adams (Eds.), *Handbook of clinical behavior therapy.* New York: Wiley, 1981.
5. SAGE PUBLICATIONS
   Forehand, R., & King, H. E. Noncompliant children: Effects of parent training on behavior and attitude change. *Behavior Modification*, 1977, *1*, 93–108.
6. SPECTRUM PUBLICATIONS
   Forehand, R., & Peed, S. Training parents to modify noncompliant behavior of their children. In A. J. Finch, Jr., & P. C. Kendall (Eds.), *Treatment and research in child psychopathology.* New York: Spectrum, 1979.

FOREWORD

Why do some children develop chronic patterns of refusal when their parents ask them to follow instructions? In one form or another, this sort of question has been voiced by clinicians for decades. However, the answers have rarely been the same from time to time. Since clinical guidelines have largely been comprised of *theory*, such fluctuation in the "state of the art" could be expected. But now, with this text by Forehand and McMahon, the field is presented a set of guidelines derived in an entirely different manner — empirical inquiry. Therein lies the unique and significant quality of *Helping the Noncompliant Child*. Theory is appropriately sparse in this presentation and, instead, we are oriented to a systematic body of data, data that offer the clinician a step-by-step understanding of child noncompliance and its resolution via parent training. This book represents a cornerstone of sound clinical practice as well as a research strategy in the solution of new clinical problems.

ROBERT G. WAHLER

PREFACE

The purpose of this book is to provide a detailed description of a treatment program designed to teach parents to modify their children's noncompliance and related deviant behavior. The program is formulated on social learning principles and is designed primarily for the parents of young (3 to 8 years of age) children. We have been extensively involved in the development and evaluation of this treatment program over the past several years. As the applicability of the program to a wide variety of problems in parent–child interaction has become evident, and its success in dealing with these problems has become more established, we have received a number of "how-to-do-it" inquiries from other professionals in the mental health field. It was these inquiries that prompted us to write this book. In addition, we sincerely hope that dissemination of our work will lead to the replication and extension of our procedures by others.

The book is intended for professionals and paraprofessionals who are involved in counseling parents of young noncompliant children. There are several prerequisites that are essential ingredients for effectively using this book. Foremost is a basic knowledge of social learning principles, child development, and an awareness of typical problems experienced by young children. In addition, experience in behavioral counseling is also desirable. We should also point out that there is some question as to whether one can read a book and then utilize its contents in a clinical situation. In training graduate students as therapists at the University of Georgia, we have used written materials in conjunction with modeling, role playing, and guided practice of the therapist skills. Discussion and verbal feedback are also extensively employed. Use of this book alone to train therapists in our treatment program has not been experimentally examined. Finally, we by no means consider our work in parent training to be conclusive. Although our research data, as presented in Chapter 6, are extensive, we hope that modification of the procedures discussed in this book and the development of new techniques will continue to occur in our laboratory as well as the laboratories of other clinical researchers.

The book is divided into six chapters. The first is designed to provide the reader with an introduction to the problem of child noncompliance, an overview of our treatment and research program, and a behavioral formulation of noncompliance. The chapter on assessment emphasizes our use of multiple measures to formulate a treatment plan and to evaluate the success of treatment in a number of areas. Chapters 3 and 4, which describe the treatment program, are clearly a most important part of this manual. In this section, we attempt to provide the reader with the information and materials necessary to conduct the parent training program. The chapter entitled "Adjunctive Treatments" presents three additions to the basic parenting program that have shown promise in facilitating positive results with families. Finally, in Chapter 6 we present a comprehensive review of our treatment research with the parent training program.

Credit for the work described in the following pages is by no means that of the authors alone. Numerous individuals have contributed to our clinical and research efforts over the past 9 years. First, Constance Hanf of the University of Oregon Medical School was our initial guiding light, as she skillfully trained the first author in many of the procedures described in this book. Second, numerous graduate students and colleagues have been instrumental in our clinical research efforts. Individuals making primary contributions include Beverly M. Atkeson, Jeri Breiner, Kenneth D. Green, Douglas L. Griest, Lewis Humphreys, H. Elizabeth King, Steve Peed, Mark W. Roberts, Tim Rogers, and Karen Wells. Thomas R. DuHamel of the Children's Orthopedic Hospital, Seattle, Washington, provided the second author (and several of his colleagues) with additional training in many of the clinical procedures described in this book. Third, the National Institute of Mental Health (NIMH) has provided funds for our research conducted during the past 4 years. Many thanks are expressed to Teri Levitin and her staff at NIMH for their financial and moral support. Fourth, a person who has received minimum recognition, but who is almost solely responsible for the daily operations of our funded research efforts, is Marilyn Steffe. Without her responsible behavior, much of the work presented in this book never would have materialized. Fifth, we are grateful to the children and their parents who approached us for help. We hope that we have improved their lives by some small measure. In return, they have suffered with us through our trial-and-error attempts and our ever-occurring battery of assessment instruments. Sixth, Kathy Stanfield's assistance in typing the many revisions of this manuscript is appreciated.

Finally, we would like to express personal thanks to several very important persons. Rex Forehand would like to thank Alfred A. Baumeister, who provided an excellent role model of an academic psychologist. Thanks also go to his parents, wife, and children — all who have taught far more about parenting and being a human being than any psychology books. Robert McMahon would like to express his appreciation to the first author of the book, who has served as an excellent role model himself, and to his wife and parents, who have offered their continued encouragement and support over the years.

CONTENTS

HELPING THE NONCOMPLIANT CHILD

1

CHILD
NONCOMPLIANCE

In THIS CHAPTER, *we present an introduction to the problem of child noncompliance by discussing the prevalence of the behavior and its implications for later adjustment. A brief overview of our parent training program for child noncompliance also is delineated, as are the therapist's ethical obligations in treating this behavior. Finally, a behavioral formulation of child noncompliance based on work by Gerald R. Patterson and by Robert G. Wahler is discussed.*

INTRODUCTION

"Jimmy will not obey me!" "Jean never comes to dinner when I call her!" "Tommy refuses to make up his bed!" "Kathy will not do anything I tell her to do!" These parental statements are familiar to professionals who engage in parent counseling and training since parents frequently complain that their children fail to comply with requests.

Numerous examples from the psychological literature on both "normal" and clinic-referred populations can be cited to illustrate the prevalence of noncompliance as a childhood behavior problem. For example, in extensive naturalistic observations in the homes of 33 nonclinic "normal" children, Johnson, Wahl, Martin, and Johansson (1973) found that among 13 "deviant" child behaviors, noncompliance was the most frequent response and occurred among more children than any other deviant behavior. Among children referred to clinics for treatment of behavior problems, noncompliance is the most frequent presenting complaint of parents (Bernal, Klinnert, & Schultz, 1980; Christophersen, Barnard, Ford, & Wolf, 1976; Patterson & Reid, 1973). For example, Bernal *et al.* (1980) reported that 35 of 36 parents who referred their children to the Family Intervention Project for treatment reported difficulties with this behavior, while Barkley (1981) indicated that noncompliance is the main problem of hyperactive children. Working with mothers of retarded children, Tavormina, Henggeler, and Gayton (1976) found that noncompliance was perceived by these parents as the most significant behavior problem they experienced with their children as well.

Consistent with these data, Johansson (1971) noted that noncompliance typically has been identified as a broad term that can include almost any type of deviant behavior. Noncompliance basically refers to the refusal to initiate or complete a request made by another person. This typically occurs when one person issues a command to another person. However, it also involves other situations in which a rule is not directly stated but is in effect. For example, many parents have a rule that children are not to jump on furniture. The parent does not have to state each day, "Do not jump on the furniture today." The rule has been stated at one point in time and does not have to be repeated daily. Using such a conceptualization of noncompliance, whining, playing with matches, fighting, destroying property, "smart-talking," and almost any other deviant behavior of a young child can be viewed as noncompliance.

Not only is noncompliance a common behavior problem, but severe manifestations of this and other similar forms of conflict between parents and young children have serious ramifications for the development of adolescent and adult psychological problems. It has been suggested that the primary developmental and experiential factors affecting the establishment of parent–child conflict occur prior to the age of 6 (Gersten, Langner, Eisenberg, Simcha-Fagen, & McCarthy, 1976). In addition, numerous studies (see Robins, 1979, for a review) have found that conduct-disorder children face a higher risk of experiencing all forms of life problems as adolescents and adults than do normal children or those who manifest other types of childhood disorders.

The frequency with which child noncompliance is perceived and experienced by parents as a problem, the broadness of its definition, and its implications for later adjustment problems if left untreated indicate the need to develop treatment procedures for this particular problem. Furthermore, such treatment should occur while the child is of preschool or early school age. As a consequence, a parenting program was developed by Dr. Constance Hanf at the University of Oregon Medical School specifically to treat child noncompliance. Subsequently, we have modified and evaluated this parent training program in a 9-year project that has involved over 100 parent–child pairs.

The parent training program (which is presented in detail in Chapters 3 and 4) makes use of a controlled learning environment (O'Dell, 1974) to teach the parent to change maladaptive patterns of interaction with the child. Sessions are conducted in a clinic setting with individual families rather than in groups. A number of discrete parenting skills are taught in a systematic manner. Therapists employ didactic instruction, modeling, and role playing with the parent. The parent also practices the skills in the clinic with the child while receiving prompting and feedback from the therapist. Finally, the parent employs these newly acquired skills in the home setting. Progression to each new skill in the treatment program is determined by the use of behavioral and temporal criteria. In this manner, an acceptable level of performance by the parent is assured. The treatment program itself consists of two phases. In the first phase of treatment, the parent is taught to be a more effective reinforcing agent for the child. The second phase of the treatment program consists of training the parent to use appropriate commands and a time-out (hereafter referred to as TO) procedure to decrease noncompliant behavior exhibited by the child.

Over 100 mother–child pairs have participated in our ongoing evaluation of the parent training program. The children, both male and female, have been referred to the University of Georgia Psychology Clinic for treatment of noncompliance and other behavior problems. Severely retarded or autistic children have not been included in this work. Referral sources have included local pediatricians, school personnel, ministers, mental health workers, and the like. The children have ranged from 3 to 8 years of age. The socioeconomic status of the families has varied from business executives and university professors to welfare recipients, with the majority of families being of a lower middle-class status.

Our approach to teaching parents to modify problem behaviors of their children has differed from some other investigators (Patterson, 1974) in that we have not made involvement of both parents[1] in the treatment program mandatory. Consequently, much of our work has been completed with mothers only. As a result of scheduling difficulties or lack of interest, fathers have attended therapy sessions in only about one-third of our cases. Intuitively, it seems that working with only part of the family is less effective than working with the entire family. Although some data are available to suggest this may not be the case (Martin, 1977), we recognize that our therapeutic approach may be less effective than it could otherwise be. Nevertheless, we have chosen to provide services to as many parents and children as possible by not excluding families in which only one parent would participate. It is hoped

---

1. This refers to families in which both the mother and father reside in the home.

that as the trend toward more equal sharing of parenting responsibilities becomes better established, fathers will become more involved.

Finally, therapists who plan to utilize the procedures described in this book should be aware of their ethical obligations when treating child noncompliance. Teaching parents to increase compliance should involve monitoring and training of parents by the therapists in regard to the kinds of commands to be given, the proper use of contingencies, and parental expectations for percentage of child compliance. For example, although unlikely, it is conceivable that parents might use the skills taught to them to obtain compliance to deviant or morally undesirable commands. Similarly, regarding the proper use of contingencies, parents may effectively reduce noncompliance by leaving a child in TO most of the day. Regarding parental expectations, parents may expect 100% compliance from their children. The normative data that have been collected and the realistic concern of parents overcontrolling their children (Peterson, 1976) would make such a goal unrealistic and harmful. It is hoped that such situations rarely occur; however, the important issue is that therapists should be sensitive to the possibility of their occurrence and incorporate instructional procedures into their training programs to prevent these situations from happening. As Risley, Clark, and Cataldo (1976) have eloquently stated, our goal should not be to develop quiet, docile children, but rather to enhance the pleasure and significance of family interactions for all members of the family.

BEHAVIORAL FORMULATION OF NONCOMPLIANCE

Behavioral formulations of the development of deviant behaviors in children have been presented by Patterson (1976a) and Wahler

(1976). Both hypotheses seem quite applicable to the development and maintenance of noncompliance in particular. Patterson emphasizes the "coercive" or controlling nature of deviant behaviors and has developed a "coercion hypothesis" to account for their development and maintenance. According to our interpretation of this hypothesis, rudimentary aversive behaviors may represent temperamental and/or developmental phenomena in the infant and young child. Regarding the former, Thomas, Chess, and Birch (1968), among others, have reported that temperamental differences (e.g., activity level, regularity of sleeping and eating, reaction to new stimuli, intensity of reaction, threshold of responsiveness, quality of mood, distractibility) exist among children in the first several months after birth. Some children display extreme behavior along each of the dimensions of temperament and, thus, are difficult to manage in the first several years of life. Regarding the latter, the developmental characteristics of the "terrible twos," during which noncompliance is prevalent, are well known. Presumably, as most infants and young children grow older, they substitute more appropriate verbal and social skills for rudimentary coercive behaviors—if the environment encourages such skills. However, according to Patterson (1976a), a number of conditions in the environment might insure that some children continue to employ aversive control strategies. For example, parents might fail to model or reinforce more appropriate prosocial skills and/or may continue to respond to the child's coercive behavior. As far as the latter point is concerned, Patterson has emphasized the role of negative reinforcement in the escalation and maintenance of coercive behaviors.

Patterson (1976a) proposes an S-R-C (aversive stimulus–child response–removal of aversive stimulus) paradigm, which, for noncompliance, can be conceptualized as parent command, child noncompliance plus other possible deviant child behaviors (e.g., negativism, yelling, crying), removal of parent command. Most researchers (Wahl, Johnson, Johansson, & Martin, 1974) have assumed that certain types of parental commands are aversive to children. The child can terminate a parental command by compliance; however, coercive behaviors such as noncompliance and negativism may also terminate the aversive parental command. Over a period of time, the deviant child learns to repeat or escalate the intensity of coercive behaviors (e.g., whining and crying) in order to terminate parental commands. The parent, in turn, may either withdraw the command, thus negatively reinforcing the noncompliance and other behaviors, or respond with coercive behaviors (e.g., yelling) of his or her own. If the latter occurs, the child may respond by complying, thus reinforcing the parental coercive behavior, or by intensifying his or her own coercive behaviors. Consequently, as a function of such experiences, parent–child interactions that are initiated by a parental command eventually are characterized by high-rate coercive *parent* and *child* behaviors, including noncompliance.

The following examples illustrate how parent and child are negatively reinforced for engaging in coercive behavior.

Application of aversive event →	*Child coercive response* →	*Removal of aversive event*
Parent gives command	Child non-complies, whines, yells	Parent gives up (withdraws the command) rather than listen to whining and screaming child

In this example, the child's coercive behaviors are negatively reinforced when the parent withdraws the aversive stimulus (command). In the following example, the coercive interchange escalates.

Application of aversive event 1 →	*Child coercive response* →	*Application of aversive event 2* →
Parent gives command	Child non-complies, whines, yells	Parent raises voice, repeats command

→ *Child response 2* →	*Application of aversive event 3* →	*Removal of child coercive response*
Child noncomplies, yells louder, kicks chair	Parent begins to yell, re-peats com-mand again	Child complies

In this example the parent's escalating coercive behavior is rein-forced by the child's eventual compliance.

It is apparent in the preceding examples how negative rein-forcement functions to increase the probability of the occurrence of deviant control techniques by both child and parent. In addi-tion, as this "training" continues over long periods of time, signifi-cant increases in rate and intensity of these coercive behaviors, including noncompliance, occur as both family members are rein-forced for a higher amplitude of deviant behavior. Thus, in this system the child is reinforced for engaging in coercive behaviors. Furthermore, the child also observes the parents engage in coercive responses, which provides the opportunity for modeling of inap-propriate behavior (Patterson, 1976a; Patterson & Reid, 1973).

Although the "negative reinforcement trap" delineated above is probably the most powerful process contributing to noncompli-ance and other deviant behaviors, Wahler (1976) has emphasized the role of positive reinforcement in also shaping these behaviors (i.e., the "positive reinforcement trap"). In this model the parent applies positive reinforcers, such as verbal or physical attention, to the child's noncompliant behaviors. In a common scenario, when instructed to go to bed, a child might refuse and throw a tantrum. A typical parental response to this act of noncompliance might be to approach the child and spend several minutes talking, trying to "understand" the child's anger, or reasoning with the child. As-suming that parental verbal attention is a reinforcing event for the child, the parent has in effect spent several minutes rewarding the very behaviors (noncompliance and tantrums) she or he is trying to eliminate. Thus, in any given situation, positive and/or negative reinforcement from the parent may be fostering the child's non-compliance.

Why do parents fall into the positive and/or negative reinforcement traps? Conger (in press) has recently provided an ecological-systems approach to family relationships that sheds some light on this issue. In this model the individual family member, the family system, and the community all contribute to the functioning of the family. Data are available indicating that each of the three factors identified by Conger may lead to child behavior problems, most likely by increasing the probability of occurrence of the parent operating within the positive and/or negative reinforcement traps. Regarding the individual family member, a relationship between parental personal adjustment (e.g., depression) and child noncompliance and other problems has been reported (Griest, Forehand, Wells, & McMahon, 1980; Johnson & Lobitz, 1974a). With respect to the family system, childhood problem behaviors are related to parental marital difficulties and to divorce (Hetherington, Cox, & Cox, 1979; Johnson & Lobitz, 1974a; Oltmanns, Broderick, & O'Leary, 1977; Porter & O'Leary, 1980). Finally, the aversiveness of the parent's interpersonal relationships in the community is related to the child's level of deviant behavior (Wahler, 1980; Wahler & Afton, 1980). In summary, factors operating within and outside the family can contribute to faulty parent-child interactions by reducing the likelihood that the parent will display effective parenting skills *and* enhancing the probability that the parent will fall into the positive and/or negative reinforcement traps.

2

ASSESSMENT

In THIS CHAPTER, *we describe the assessment measures used in our parent training program. An overview of the assessment procedures is followed by a description of the interview, the questionnaires that are completed by parents, the parental recording of child behaviors in the home, and the direct observation procedures by independent observers in the clinic and home.*

AN OVERVIEW

The role of assessment in the treatment of problem behaviors is receiving increasing attention, as is evident by the recent appearance of two journals *(Behavioral Assessment* and *Journal of Behavioral Assessment)* as well as numerous books devoted to the topic (Ciminero, Calhoun, & Adams, 1977; Haynes, 1978; Mash & Terdal, 1981). Assessment serves many functions, including the determination as to whether a problem actually exists, the identification of a proper treatment procedure, and the determination of the effectiveness of treatment. We place a major emphasis on the assessment of the noncompliant child and his or her family through the use of multiple instruments. These include interviews, parent-completed questionnaires, parent-recorded data, and direct observations in the clinic and home by independent observers.

Although there is some overlap among the various assessment modalities with respect to the type of information they provide, each modality provides unique information on some aspect of the parent–child interaction. By assessing the child and parent(s) by multiple procedures, we are more likely to identify the problem behaviors and their controlling events (Atkeson & Forehand, 1978, 1981).

Each of the assessment measures has its own advantages and disadvantages. The advantages of each type of assessment are presented in the sections that follow. The problems have been delineated by a number of investigators (Evans & Nelson, 1977; Hersen & Barlow, 1976; Kent & Foster, 1977; Lipinski & Nelson, 1974) and are summarized briefly here. Difficulties associated with the use of independent observers to collect behavioral data include (1) loss of information with the use of a coding system, (2) the necessity of assessing and calculating reliability, (3) questionable stability of data, (4) observer error, (5) subject reactivity to being observed, and (6) setting instructions (e.g., "Do not watch television and avoid having visitors during the observation"). With questionnaires and interviews, demand characteristics, impression management, and unidirectional responding are among the limitations. Finally, with parent-collected data all the disadvantages of data collected by independent observers are applicable as well as the demand characteristics and impression management problems associated with questionnaires. Despite these difficulties, we agree with Johnson and Eyberg (1975), who state that "no one class of assessment instruments can adequately reflect change in complex human processes. All types are fallible and worthy in different respects, and each may best be employed to complement, clarify, and correct for the others" (p. 918). This statement accurately reflects our philosophy regarding assessment for the parent training program.

The four sections of this chapter that follow present the assessment procedures and instruments we utilize as part of our parent

training program. The majority of the initial assessment procedures occur at the first meeting with the family. The parent is asked
to note his or her chief concerns about the child on the Parent Behavior Checklist. Most of the initial session consists of the parent
interview, which lasts approximately 45 minutes. The remainder
of the session is taken up with a 10-minute observation of the parent–child interaction, a brief interview with the child (approximately 5 to 10 minutes), and making arrangements for the remaining assessment procedures (15 minutes). These include the parent
selection of problem behaviors to record in the home, arranging a
home observation time, and giving questionnaires to the parent to
complete at home. The time required for each segment of the assessment will obviously vary depending upon any of a number of
factors (e.g., complexity of problems, age of the child, intelligence
of parents). We typically allow 1 ½ to 2 hours for the initial assessment session.

THE INTERVIEW

The interview is the first contact the therapist has with the child
and his or her parent(s). The primary function of the interview is to
identify verbally the behaviors to be targeted for treatment and the
conditions, both antecedent and consequent, currently maintaining the problem behaviors. The interview focuses on both adult
and child behaviors and, more specifically, on the pattern of interaction between the child and adult. As a consequence, the responses identified for treatment during the interview include parent and
child behaviors.

Although the major purpose of an interview from a behavioral
viewpoint is to determine factors currently operating to maintain
the problem interactions, the initial contact with significant adults
in the child's life can have other, quite important functions (Ciminero & Drabman, 1977; Evans & Nelson, 1977; Haynes, 1978). In

addition to gathering current data, a second purpose of the initial interview is to obtain a developmental history of the problem interactions. While rarely useful in designing a treatment program, a developmental history of the problem parent-child interactions may be helpful in the following ways: (1) it may suggest conditions under which the problem behavior may reappear after successful modification; (2) it may provide information concerning controlling variables; (3) it may promote understanding for the client of how behavior problems begin; and (4) the historical information may be relevant to the development of preventive programs (Haynes, 1978). In addition, a developmental history of the interactional problems provides the therapist with a better understanding of the extent and severity of the problem behaviors. For example, as noted in the preceding chapter, temperamental factors may be operating to produce a problem situation that has existed since the first few months of life.

A third function of the initial interview is to assess both the motivation of the parent for working in therapy and his or her ability to understand and execute behavioral programs. Closely related to this is the fourth function: clear communication to the parent of the conceptual framework of the therapist and the nature of the intervention process. Fifth, the initial interview is the first, and perhaps most important, opportunity for the therapist to develop a rapport with both the parent and child. Unless the parent is highly motivated, can understand and execute programs, is receptive to the therapy approach, and has a positive, trusting relationship with the therapist, attempts to implement the therapy program will be futile. Finally, the initial interview can provide the therapist with the opportunity to question the parent about the need for a medical, speech, or auditory evaluation of the child. Our experience has suggested that neurological difficulties, mild hearing impairments, and language delays may occasionally be occurring in children referred to clinics for the treatment of noncompliance. If the therapist suspects any of these problems, an appropriate referral (i.e., physician, speech therapist, audiologist) should occur prior to the initiation of parent training.

Interview with the Parents

There are two considerations concerning the initial interview that must be dealt with before the family even walks through the door. The first has to do with who should be present at the interview. We always have at least one parent and the child come to the clinic. There are very real advantages to attempting to have both parents (as well as the child) attend at least the initial interview. First of all, it allows the therapist to obtain a more complete picture of the patterns of interaction between each parent and the child, the degree of consistency (or, as is more often the case, inconsistency) between parents in their childrearing philosophy and behavior, and a behavioral sample of the marital interaction. Such information may prove invaluable in the implementation of the parenting program. The second advantage to having both parents present at the initial interview is that it may provide a "foot in the door" to having the unwilling parent (usually the father) participate in the parenting program (LaBarbera & Lewis, 1980). We have found that many fathers allow themselves to be persuaded to become involved in the parenting program to at least some degree after they have attended the initial interview and after the conceptualization of the presenting problem and the rationale of the program have been presented to them. It seems that following the assessment procedures and the presentation of the conceptualization and rationale, many of these fathers are quite pleased to find that the program makes sense to them. We have had numerous cases in which both parents have reported their relief at finding that the program would not involve "shrink stuff" (e.g., couches), and that it is skill-oriented and "practical." Thus, by having both parents attend the initial session(s), valuable information may be obtained, and, it is hoped, both parents can be persuaded of the importance of having complete parental participation in the program.

The second consideration concerns whether the child will remain in the room during the parent interview. As a general rule, we prefer to interview the parent(s) alone at the initial interview. Although the child's presence provides the therapist with an opportunity to observe the child's behavior and the parent's reaction to it, this information is best gathered in the more standardized setting of the clinic and home observations. We have found that a "private" session without the child allows the parent to discuss the relationship with his or her child more freely without fear of the child overhearing. In addition, it avoids the situation where the child excessively disrupts the interview process. When the child's disruptive behavior occurs repeatedly in the early stages of the initial interview, the parent may become excessively embarrassed. Such a reaction, as well as the disruptive behavior itself, mitigate against the development of rapport between therapist and parent. It is necessary, then, to have someone watch (and perhaps interview and play with) the child in the waiting room or in an adjacent therapy room. The therapist can then interview the child (as is described later) following completion of the behavioral interview with the parent.

Occasionally, space and/or personnel limitations may require that the child remain in the room during the initial interview. When this happens, some toys can be provided, and the child can be instructed by the parent to "play with the toys while I talk to Dr. _____." We usually observe how the parent handles the child's positive and negative behaviors during the first few minutes. If the parent has difficulty with the child's behavior (which is why they are in our office in the first place!), we generally assume the disciplinary role for the duration of the interview. In this manner, we provide the parent with early examples of some of the skills he or she will be learning. Obviously, this must be done in such a manner as to avoid making the parent feel inadequate. A reassuring statement such as, "I know it's hard to handle kids when they're in a new place" will usually be sufficient.

Regarding the content of the interview, the therapist first obtains written consent from the parent for both the parent and the child to be treated. Inasmuch as the rest of the first session and considerable intersession time will be devoted to the collection of assessment data, it is important to present the parent with a rationale for the necessity of obtaining this information. We stress that the assessment data will allow us to direct our treatment to the most appropriate targets and that this information will also be of direct benefit in informing us of our effectiveness. If the receptionist has not already done so, the therapist then obtains demographic information concerning the child and family. This includes such data as the child's date of birth, grade in school, and number of siblings; the siblings' sex and grade in school; and the parents' age, education, and occupation. Having obtained this information, the therapist is ready to pursue the major purpose of the initial interview: the assessment of the nature of the typical parent–child interactions that are problems, the antecedent stimulus conditions under which problem behaviors occur, and the consequences that accompany such behaviors.

The interview itself typically begins with a general question, such as, "Tell me what types of problems you have been having with _____," or "What brings you to the clinic?" By beginning the interview in this manner, the therapist is provided with an immediate opportunity to hear the parent's major concerns about the child and to obtain some initial feeling as to his or her perception of the type of treatment he or she is seeking. With respect to the latter point, it is often at this time that the "Play-Therapy Parent" (see Chapter 4) reveals expectations that if the child is dropped off at the clinic, the therapist will "fix" the problem, and the child can be picked up an hour later.

In our experience, most parents, not surprisingly, respond

globally to the general question about the types of problems they are experiencing with their children. To structure the interview and the information obtained from the parent concerning current parent–child problem interactions, the therapist examines the antecedent conditions of the situation ("What happens just before the problem interaction?"), the child's behavior ("What does _____ do?"), the parent's response ("What do you do?"), and the child's reaction to the parent's intervention ("What does _____ do then?"). The analysis of both the parent's and child's behavior in the problem situation should be continued until the therapist has a clear understanding of the nature and extent of the parent–child interaction. Other relevant information, such as the frequency ("How often . . . ? "), duration ("How long . . . ? "), and historical–developmental questions specific to the problem interaction should also be gathered.

Once a clear description of the parent-delineated problems is obtained, the therapist presents a number of situations that may or may not be problem areas in which noncompliance and other deviant behaviors exist for the particular family. The parent is asked if the child is noncompliant or disruptive in situations such as the following: visiting in a friend's home, riding in the car, shopping, adult–adult conversations, parental telephone conversations, homework, cleaning up, naptime, bath time and bedtime. Information is also elicited with respect to whether the child experiences behavioral or academic difficulties in school, and the child's relationships with other family members as well as peers. If the parent reports that a particular behavior or setting is not a problem, the therapist moves to the next situation. If the parent reports that a particular situation is a problem area for him or her, then the therapist, proceeding in a manner similar to that described, attempts to delineate both parent and child behaviors that are occurring in the situation. Finally, the parent is questioned about the disciplinary procedures he or she is currently using with the child. An open-ended question ("How do you discipline _____?") is used to initiate questioning in this area. Frequency, duration (if applicable), and parent and child responses to the disciplinary act can be examined.

Figure 2.1 presents a sample problem guidesheet for interviewing parents. In addition to providing a more complete picture of the interaction pattern between parent and child, this interview format also acquaints parents with the behavioral orientation of the therapist.

The following is a portion of an initial interview to exemplify the analysis of a problem situation.

THERAPIST: Do you have any problems with Mark at bedtime?

PARENT: Oh my gosh, yes. It takes forever for him to go to sleep. He gets out of bed again and again.

THERAPIST: Tell me about your family's routine during the half-hour before Mark's bedtime.

PARENT: At 7:30 I help Mark with his bath. After he brushes his teeth and goes to the bathroom, I read him a story. Then Bob and I kiss him goodnight and tell him to stay in bed and to go to sleep.

THERAPIST: OK, then what happens?

PARENT: Well, things are quiet for about 10–15 minutes. Then Mark is up. He gets out of bed and comes into the den where Bob and I are watching tv.

THERAPIST: What does Mark do when he gets up?

PARENT: He usually comes in and climbs in either Bob's or my lap and complains that he can't sleep.

THERAPIST: What do you do then?

PARENT: Sometimes we let him sit with us for a while but usually I take him back to bed, tell him goodnight again, and tell him to stay in bed.

THERAPIST: What happens then?

PARENT: Mark stays there for a while but he's soon out again.

THERAPIST: And then what do you do?

FIG. 2.1. PROBLEM GUIDESHEET

Child: Interviewer(s):
Interviewee(s):   Date:

Setting	Description	Frequency	Duration	Parent Response	Child Response
Bedtime (A.M. and P.M.)					
Mealtime					
Bath time					
On phone					
Visitors — at home					
Visiting others					
Car					
Public places (stores, etc.)					
School					
Siblings					
Peers					
Other parent/ relative					
Discipli- nary pro- cedures					
Other					

PARENT: I may tell him he's being a bad boy. Then I take him back to bed. Usually I read him another story — hoping he'll get sleepy this time.

THERAPIST: Does that work?

PARENT: No, he's up again before I have time to get settled in my chair.

THERAPIST: What happens then?

PARENT: The whole thing repeats itself. I put him in bed, read him another story, and he gets up again.

THERAPIST: How long does this go on?

PARENT: For about 2 or 3 hours — until Bob and I go to bed.

THERAPIST: What happens when you and your husband go to bed?

PARENT: Mark still gets up but we let him get in bed with us and he goes to sleep then.

THERAPIST: How many nights a week does this happen?

PARENT: Every night! I can't think of a night's peace in the last few months.

THERAPIST: How long has Mark been doing this?

PARENT: Oh, I would guess for about a year.

THERAPIST: Have you or your husband tried any other ways of handling Mark at bedtime?

PARENT: Sometimes I get angry and yell at him. Sometimes Bob tries spanking him but then Mark just ends up crying all evening. At least my way we have a little peace and quiet.

In this sample interview, the therapist obtained a description of the events preceding the problem situation fairly quickly. The therapist had to repeat "What happens then?" or some variation thereof, several times until a clear description of the consequent events currently maintaining the problem behavior was obtained. Based on this assessment, the problem behavior — noncompliance at bedtime (getting out of bed) — is occurring at a high rate and has been for some time.

The next sample interview centers around the same problem situation, bedtime; in this clinical case the antecedent events emerged as important factors maintaining the problem interaction.

THERAPIST: Do you have a problem with Jimmy at bedtime?

PARENT: Certainly! He's impossible. He starts to scream and cry the minute we put him to bed.

THERAPIST: Tell me about your family's routine the half-hour before Jimmy's bedtime.

PARENT: Well, Jimmy takes his bath and puts on his pajamas right after supper. Then we usually watch television together. He knows his bedtime is 8:30, so when the program ends, his father says, "Bedtime." Then the problems begin. Jimmy trys to stall, begging to see the next show. We ignore this. His father usually ends up carrying Jimmy—screaming all the way—to bed.

THERAPIST: What happens then?

PARENT: He used to get up again and again. Each time we would spank him and put him back to bed. Now when we put him to bed the first time we just lock his door. He crys for a while and then drops off to sleep.

THERAPIST: How many nights a week does this happen?

PARENT: Let me see. Nearly all the time.

THERAPIST: Thinking back over the past week, how many nights out of the last seven have you had problems with Jimmy at bedtime?

PARENT: Hmmm. Four.

THERAPIST: How long has Jimmy been difficult at bedtime?

PARENT: For the last 6 months.

Based on this interview, the therapist concluded that the antecedent events (the abrupt announcement of bedtime and removal of the child to bed) were contributing to the child's problem behaviors at bedtime.

After the therapist has determined the situations that are currently problems for the parent and child and the antecedent and
consequent factors maintaining these problematic parent-child
interactions, a brief developmental history of the child is obtained.
The developmental history should cover difficulties during preg-
nancy, birth, and early childhood; the ages for developmental
milestones, such as sitting, standing, walking, and talking; medical, speech, and hearing problems; and the presence/absence of
various toileting problems. The therapist may choose to pursue the
existence of early temperamental characteristics (Thomas *et al.*,
1968). These include activity level, rhythmicity (regularity of
sleeping, eating, etc.), approach to or withdrawal from new stimuli, adaptability to new situations, intensity of reaction, threshold of
responsiveness, quality of mood, distractibility, and attention
span. Thomas, Chess, Birch, Hertzig, and Korn (1963) have published criteria and methods for assessing these temperamental
characteristics.

It is important to note that the therapist's clinical skills are important in the initial interview. Clearly, the behavioral interview is
quite structured as substantial information is being obtained in a
brief period of time. However, within this context the therapist
must be warm, genuine, sensitive, and responsive to the individual
parent's needs. Our subjective experience is that the therapist's
clinical skills in the initial interview play an essential role in determining whether or not a parent will return for treatment.

Interview with the Child

We have found an individual interview with children 5 years of age
and younger to be of limited value in providing the therapist with
content information. Even with younger children, however, a few
minutes spent privately with the child in a play situation or a walk
to the pop machine allows the therapist to obtain a sample of how
the child interacts with an unfamiliar adult in a social situation

(Evans & Nelson, 1977) and to assess the child's perception of why the child has been brought to the clinic.

With children of all ages the therapist typically begins with the statement "Tell me why you are here today." We have often been surprised at the range of responses this has elicited, from a realistic appraisal of "So Mommy and Daddy and I don't fight so much," to the more typical one of "I don't know," to more interesting statements such as "So I'll have someone to play with." After the child has responded, it is helpful to explain to the child your view of why he or she is at the clinic. The explanation might be, "Your parents are concerned because you and they don't seem to be getting along very well. They came to see us to get some help so things will be more pleasant for you and them at home."

The interview, particularly with older children, can provide the therapist with additional pertinent information. The therapist asks the child about various situations at home or elsewhere in an attempt to obtain the child's perception about what is happening in these problem situations. Sometimes such questioning is fruitless; at other times the child's understanding of the situation and the role he or she plays is quite accurate. Such statements as "I know if I say dirty words that Dad goes to pieces and then Mom gets involved" can be quite informative. Some general areas for questioning include family issues (e.g., "What kinds of things do you do with your father/mother/brothers/sisters?" "What can you do to make your father/mother happy/mad?"), school (e.g., "Tell me about school" "What do you like best at school?" "What do you dislike most at school?"), social activities (e.g., "Tell me about your friends" "What kinds of things do you do with [friend's name]?"), and personal preferences (e.g., "What are your favorite things?" "What do you like to do most?"). In addition to content information, this semistructured interview with the child provides the therapist with a more thorough subjective evaluation of the child's cognitive level and behavioral characteristics (e.g., verbal and social skills).

PARENT-COMPLETED QUESTIONNAIRES

Questionnaires that parents complete as part of the assessment process can give the therapist additional information beyond that obtained in the interview. For example, due to time limitations, the therapist may not be able to explore all relevant areas. Questionnaires completed by parents allow the therapist to examine some of these areas. Of most importance, the completion of the questionnaires does not require any time commitment from the therapist. They are simply given to the parent at the end of the initial interview and the parent is asked to complete them and return them prior to or at the next session. If the therapist notes particular areas of concern from the parent's responses on the questionnaire, these can be explored in the second session. This is particularly true for parental personal and marital adjustment. As the initial interview focuses on parent-child problem interactions, the personal and marital adjustment of the parent may not be examined. Questionnaires concerning such adjustment can provide the therapist with important information for discussion in subsequent sessions.

Questionnaires are also important in that they measure parental perceptions. Our other assessment instruments (e.g., behavioral observations) may indicate that a child is not noncompliant and deviant; however, the parent may report on a questionnaire that the child is perceived as noncompliant and deviant at home. This tells the therapist that it is not the child's behavior, but rather the parent's expectations that need to be changed. Data from some of our recent investigations indicate that this situation occurs with some frequency (see Chapter 6). Questionnaires that tap parental perceptions of the child also provide valuable information concerning the social validity of the treatment program, that is, whether the child's behavior is considered to be improved after treatment by significant individuals in the child's environment. Chapter 6 describes our examination of the social validity of the parent training program.

We use parent-completed questionnaires to assess four areas: parental perceptions of child adjustment; parental perceptions of their own personal and marital adjustment; parental knowledge of social learning principles; and parental satisfaction with treatment. Questionnaires in the first three areas are given to the parent to complete at the end of the initial assessment session. They should be returned to the clinic (by the parent, home observer, or mail) prior to or at the beginning of the next session so that the therapist can determine whether additional assessment in these areas is warranted. These questionnaires, as well as the one in the fourth area, can also be given to the parent to complete after treatment is terminated and at follow-up assessments. Because of the young age of the treated children, we have not used questionnaires with them.

If possible, it is most helpful to have both parents complete the questionnaires. Areas of discrepancy and mutual agreement between parents are an important source of data, whether they concern perceptions of the child's behavior or the marital relationship. In addition, responses to questionnaires by both parents may suggest differential therapeutic goals for the two parents. For example, treatment for depression concomitantly with parent training may be necessary for the father, while extensive training in social learning principles may be beneficial for the mother. It is important to have each parent complete the questionnaires separately. This is both to maintain independence of responding and to provide confidentiality. This latter consideration is most relevant with the measures of personal adjustment and marital satisfaction. For these two measures it is important to tell the parents that some of the questions touch on personal matters and, consequently, that confidentiality will be provided.

Parent Perceptions of Child Adjustment

The Parent Attitudes Test (PAT) (Cowen, Huser, Beach, & Rappaport, 1970) has been our primary measure of parent perceptions of child adjustment.[1] Three subscales — Home Attitude Scale, Behavior Rating Scale, and Adjective Checklist Scale — from the PAT are typically administered. (The School Attitude Scale can be administered also; however, because of the young age of many of the children, we usually have not utilized this scale.) The Home Attitude Scale consists of seven items that reflect the parent's perception of the child's adjustment in the home. The Behavior Rating Scale consists of 23 items, each of which refers to a behavior problem, while the Adjective Checklist Scale consists of 34 adjectives, each describing a child behavior or personality characteristic. Cowen et al. (1970) have presented evidence demonstrating the reliability and validity of these scales. Furthermore, each of the scales differentiates parents of nonclinic and clinic-referred children (Forehand, King, Peed, & Yoder, 1975; Griest et al., 1980) and demonstrates positive change with implementation of the parent training program (e.g., Forehand & King, 1977; Forehand, Wells, & Griest, 1980).

It is important to note, as is discussed in Chapter 6, that even parents who were assigned to a waiting-list control group (and consequently received no treatment for a 5-week period) reported some degree of positive change in their children on several of the scales (Peed, Roberts, & Forehand, 1977). This occurred despite the lack of corresponding improvement in child behavior during home observations. Therefore, parental perceptions of child adjustment, while an important aspect of parent–child interaction, are probably not an adequate criterion for assessing child behavior problems or evaluating the outcome of therapy if employed alone.

The PAT is available from Emory L. Cowen, Psychology Department, University of Rochester, Rochester, New York 14627.

1. We have employed the Patterson and Fagot (1967) abridged version of the Becker Bipolar Adjective Checklist (Becker, 1960) in some of our previous work. As we rely less on this instrument now, it will not be presented. For information on this measure, the reader is referred to Patterson, Reid, Jones, and Conger (1975).

Parent Perceptions of Personal Adjustment
and Marital Satisfaction

The Beck Depression Inventory (Beck, Rush, Shaw, & Emery, 1979) has been our primary measure of parental perceptions of personal adjustment, while the modified form of Locke's Marital Adjustment Test (Kimmel & van der Veen, 1974) has been the instrument used to measure parents' perceptions of marital satisfaction. Both measures are readily administered and scored.

The Beck scores correlate significantly with clinicians' ratings of depression (Metcalfe & Goldman, 1965) and with objective behavioral measures of depression (Williams, Barlow, & Agras, 1972). Furthermore, the inventory differentiates parents of clinic-referred and nonclinic children (Griest et al., 1980) and demonstrates positive changes with the implementation of our parent training program (Forehand et al., 1980). The Beck inventory consists of 21 items, each of which is scored as 0, 1, 2, or 3. A higher score indicates more depression. Beck has delineated the following cutoff points: 0-9, no depression or minimal depression; 10-14, borderline depression; 15-20, mild depression; 21-30, moderate depression; 31-40, severe depression; 41-63, very severe depression. The questionnaire is presented in Beck et al. (1979) or may be obtained from the Center for Cognitive Therapy, Room 602, 133 South 36th Street, Philadelphia, Pennsylvania 19104.

Locke's Marital Adjustment Test is a questionnaire that has been used in much of the clinical research on marital discord. It is a reliable instrument that has been shown to discriminate between distressed and nondistressed couples (Locke & Wallace, 1959). Furthermore, marital distress as measured by the Marital Adjustment Test has been found to be significantly correlated with deviant child behavior (Johnson & Lobitz, 1974a). Finally, a slightly modified form of the test yields scores that are stable over an extended period of time (i.e., 2¼ years) (Kimmel & van der Veen, 1974). The modified version of the questionnaire consists of 44 weighted items. A high score on the questionnaire indicates a greater degree of marital satisfaction. The following means and standard deviations were obtained by Kimmel and van der Veen for a sample of 149 wives and 157 husbands: wives—mean = 108.40, SD = 16.32; husbands—mean = 110.22, SD = 16.28.

The questionnaire and scoring instructions are presented in Kimmel and van der Veen (1974).

Parent Knowledge of Social Learning Principles

In order to determine the parents' knowledge of social learning principles, we began administering a slightly abridged version of the Knowledge of Behavioral Principles as Applied to Children (KBPAC) test (O'Dell, Tarler-Benlolo, & Flynn, 1979). Our recent work (McMahon, Forehand, & Griest, 1981) indicates that parents who receive formal instruction in the social learning principles underlying our treatment program tend to be more satisfied with treatment, generalize their skills more effectively, and perceive their children more positively than parents who are not explicitly taught the principles (see Chapters 5 and 6). The KBPAC provides a basic measure of the level of sophistication the parent brings to the treatment program with regard to knowledge of social learning principles. With the use of this instrument, the therapist can determine to what extent social learning principles need to be presented to the parent.

The abridged KBPAC consists of 45 multiple-choice questions, most of which present practical problem situations. Each question has four possible answers. The parent is asked to select the response that is the most likely to produce the desired effect. A total score is obtained by summing the number of items answered correctly. O'Dell et al. (1979) have presented preliminary reliability and validity data.

The KBPAC and scoring key are presented in O'Dell et al. (1979).

Parent Satisfaction with Treatment

A Parent's Consumer Satisfaction Questionnaire has been developed recently to measure parental satisfaction with treatment received in our parent training program. Several investigators (Kazdin, 1977; Wolf, 1978) have suggested that consumer satisfaction with a particular treatment strategy or an entire treatment approach is likely to be a factor in the ultimate effectiveness of the intervention. As noted earlier, the consumer satisfaction measure is administered at the end of the treatment program as well as at subsequent follow-ups. Recent data (McMahon, Forehand, & Griest, 1981) indicate that parents do perceive the program positively. The measure samples parent satisfaction with the overall program, the teaching format, the specific parenting techniques taught, and the therapists. Items examining both the usefulness and difficulty of the teaching format and specific parenting techniques are included. In all of the areas, parents respond to items on a 7-point Likert scale. Parents also have the opportunity to reply to several open-ended questions concerning their reactions to the parenting program.

The Parent's Consumer Satisfaction Questionnaire and a key for scoring are presented in Appendix A.

PARENT-RECORDED BEHAVIOR

One approach to obtaining information about child noncompliant and deviant behaviors is to have the parent record the frequency of the behaviors in the home. Parental recording of the child's behavior offers several advantages over other assessment procedures. First, it gives more precise information about the child's behavior than an interview or parent-completed questionnaire. Second, relative to behavioral observations completed by independent observers, it is efficient. Third, with certain low-rate behaviors such as stealing and fire-setting, it may be the only way to obtain information on the occurrence of these behaviors.

At the beginning of the initial interview, the parent completes the Parent Behavior Checklist, which is presented in Figure 2.2. The 11 problem behaviors listed on that checklist have been identified as aversive child behaviors as determined by parental ratings and the parental consequences applied to the behaviors (Adkins & Johnson, 1972). As indicated in the instructions to the checklist, the parent is asked to check the behaviors that present problem areas with the child and then rank the problem behaviors that are of the most concern to him or her in order of their severity. The information can then be used in the interview as an additional problem guide. At the conclusion of the interview, the behaviors receiving the top three ranks are carefully defined jointly by the therapist and parent. As indicated in the instruction sheet pre-

---

FIG. 2.2. PARENT BEHAVIOR CHECKLIST

Check the behaviors below that represent problem areas with your child. Then rank-order the behaviors you checked from primary problem (rank of 1) to least problem.

_____ 1. Whine

_____ 2. Physical negative (attacks another person)

_____ 3. Humiliate (makes fun of, shames, or embarrasses others)

_____ 4. Destructiveness (destroys, damages, or attempts to damage any object)

_____ 5. Tease

_____ 6. Smart talk

_____ 7. Noncompliance (does not do what he or she is told to do)

_____ 8. Ignore (fails to answer)

_____ 9. Yell

_____ 10. Demand attention

_____ 11. Temper tantrum

---

sented in Figure 2.3, the parent then is asked to record the frequency of each of the three selected problem behaviors during the 24-hour periods prior to each of the four home observations. For recording purposes the parent is given index cards that list the three behaviors. The completed card is given to the observer each day. (If home observations are not conducted, the parent can be requested to record for four consecutive 24-hour periods and to bring the data cards to the first treatment session.)

The therapist then can use this information to identify the frequency of the reported problem behaviors. The information can also be used in subsequent sessions with the parent to discuss particular incidents of child problem behaviors, as well as the relvant antecedent conditions and consequences. The same parent-recorded data can be collected after treatment and at any follow-ups to assess changes resulting from treatment.

DIRECT OBSERVATION

Direct behavioral observation by independent, well-trained observers is the most accepted procedure for obtaining a reliable and valid description of current parent–child interactions. Through the appropriate use of behavioral observation, the therapist is able to obtain measures on the frequency and duration of child problem behaviors and the relationship between child and parent behaviors and, thus, is able to quantify the problem interactions targeted for treatment.

Observations may occur in either the home or the clinic setting. While extremely valuable for assessment and treatment, behavioral observations by independent observers in the home are very expensive and time-consuming — that is, they lack efficiency. An alternative assessment procedure, which certainly reduces the time and cost required for observation in the natural setting, is the

FIG. 2.3. COUNTING YOUR CHILD'S BEHAVIOR

One of the things we have asked you to do is to keep track of several of your child's behaviors for 4 days. As we explained, this will help us to design a better treatment program for you and help determine its effectiveness. Therefore, it is very important that you try to be as accurate as possible. The attached index cards and envelopes are each numbered 1 to 4. Also, note that each index card lists three behaviors. These are the behaviors that you listed earlier as being of concern to you. We would like you to do the following:

1. For the 24-hour period *before* each of the four home observations, keep a running tab of the number of times your child does each of these three behaviors. Most parents find that carrying the index card in a pocket or putting it in a conspicuous place (for example, on the refrigerator door) is a good way to remind themselves to record this information. Simply put a slash or a number down on the card each time the behavior occurs. An example of day 3's results might look like this:

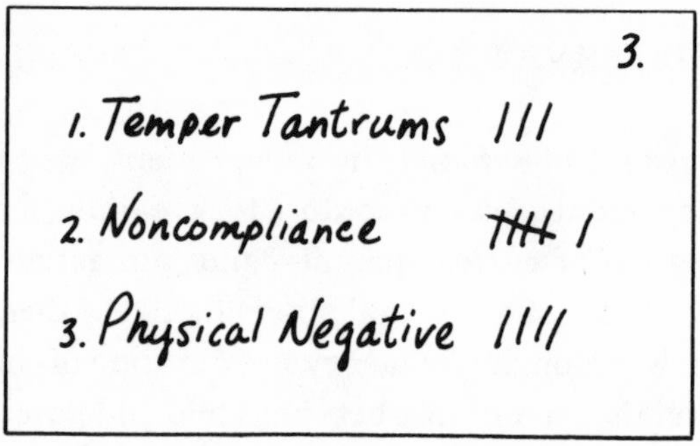

```
                                              3.

   1. Temper Tantrums   ///

   2. Noncompliance      ////  /

   3. Physical Negative  ////
```

Try to make sure the time period you record for is 24 hours — no more, no less.

2. Place the card in the envelope and seal it.

3. When the observer comes to your home, give him or her the envelope.

4. Remember to keep track of these same behaviors for the 24-hour period before each home observation.

Thanks!

observation of parent–child interactions in a structured setting in the clinic. Use of a structured clinic observation is advantageous for several reasons: (1) it efficiently elicits the problematic parent–child interactions; (2) observation can occur unobtrusively through one-way windows; (3) the standard situation allows the therapist to make within- and between-client comparisons (Hughes & Haynes, 1978). Unfortunately, the validity of the information obtained in a clinic setting is sometimes questionable (Martin, Johnson, Johansson, & Wahl, 1976). We have found it best to use both clinic and home observations. These assessment procedures are described in this section.

Coding System

We have developed an observational system for use in both the clinic and home settings (Forehand, Peed, Roberts, McMahon, Griest, & Humphreys, 1978). The coding system was designed specifically to tap patterns of parent–child interaction as well as specific parent and child behaviors. The coding manual used to train observers for this system is presented in Appendix B. The training procedure, which is no easy matter, will be discussed later in this chapter. A brief definition of each of the parent and child behaviors that are recorded will be presented here.

The parent behaviors are the following:

1. Rewards: praise, approval, or positive physical attention that refers to the child or the child's activity; verbal rewards include both specific (labeled) and nonspecific (unlabeled) reference to "praiseworthy" behavior.
2. Attends: descriptive phrases that follow and refer to (a) the child's ongoing behavior, (b) objects directly related to the child's play, (c) his or her spatial position (e.g., "You're standing in the middle of the room"), or (d) appearance of the child.
3. Questions: interrogatives to which the only appropriate response is verbal.
4. Commands

    a. Alpha commands: an order, rule, suggestion, or question to which a motoric response is appropriate and feasible.

    b. Beta commands: commands to which the child has no opportunity to demonstrate compliance. Beta commands include parental commands that are (1) so vague that proper action for compliance cannot be determined, (2) interrupted by further parental verbiage before enough time (5 seconds) has elapsed for the child to comply, or (3) carried out by the parent before the child has an opportunity to comply. A beta command is also scored if the parent restricts the child's mobility in such a way as to preclude a compliance opportunity.

5. Warnings: statements that describe aversive consequences to be delivered by the parent if the child fails to comply to a parental command.

6. Time-out: a procedure used by the parent that clearly is intended to remove the child from positive reinforcement because of the child's inappropriate behaviors (e.g., placing the child in a chair in the corner of the room).

The child behaviors are the following:

1. Child compliance: an appropriate motoric response initiated within 5 seconds following a parental alpha command.

2. Child noncompliance: failure to initiate a motoric response within 5 seconds following a parental alpha command.

3. Child inappropriate (other deviant) behavior: behaviors that include (a) whining, crying, yelling, and tantrums, (b) aggression (e.g., biting, kicking, hitting, slapping, grabbing an object from someone, or the threat of aggression), and (c) deviant talk (e.g., repetitive requests for attention, stated refusals to comply, disrespectful statements, profanity, and commands to parents that threaten aversive consequences).

Data are recorded in 30-second intervals. Behaviors are scored sequentially as they occur in each interval. The single exception is inappropriate behavior, which is recorded on an occurrence/nonoccurrence basis for each 30-second interval.

Some data are available pertaining to the reliability and validity of the coding system. With respect to reliability, Forehand and Peed (1979) reported an average interobserver agreement of 75%. The coding system possesses adequate test–retest reliability as well. Data from repeated observations of nonintervention parent–child interactions are stable and consistent (Peed et al., 1977).

The next question concerns the validity of the instrument. Using the coding system, Forehand et al. (1975) and Griest et al. (1980) found significant differences in compliance between clinic-referred and nonclinic-referred children. The observation procedure is also sensitive enough to measure significant treatment effects in the clinic and home with a clinic-referred population (Forehand, Griest, & Wells, 1979; Forehand, Sturgis, McMahon, Aguar, Green, Wells, & Breiner, 1979; Humphreys, Forehand, McMahon, & Roberts, 1978; Peed et al., 1977). In other studies, parent–child interactions in the clinic have been shown to be similar to those observed in the home (Peed et al., 1977) and to predict child behavior in the home (Forehand, Wells, & Sturgis, 1978). More specifically, treatment effects observed in the clinic coincide with treatment effects observed in the home (Peed et al., 1977).

Clinic Observations

Following the interview, the parent–child pair is observed in a clinic playroom equipped with a one-way observation window and wired for sound. The playroom contains various age-appropriate toys, such as building blocks, toy trucks and cars, dolls, puzzles, crayons, and paper. Prior to the clinic observation, the parent is instructed to interact with the child in two different contexts, referred to as the Child's Game and the Parent's Game. In the Child's Game, the parent is instructed to engage in any activity that the child chooses and to allow the child to determine the nature and rules of the interaction. Thus, the Child's Game is essentially a free-play situation. In the Parent's Game, the parent is instructed to engage the child in activities whose rules and nature are determined by the parent. The Parent's Game is essentially a command situation.

It is important to note that sometimes a parent will be hesitant about interacting with the child while being observed. The therapist should assure the parent that these feelings are normal but that it is important to obtain a sample of how the child interacts with the parent. It also is important for the therapist to tell the parent that it is recognized that such an interaction between parent and child will be artificial; nevertheless, it will provide some meaningful information.

The clinic observation consists of coding the parent–child interaction from behind a one-way observation window for 5 minutes in both Child's and Parent's Games. (If a one-way observation window is not available, the observer can sit in a corner of the playroom and code the interaction.) Following the clinic observation, the data are summarized for both the Child's Game and Parent's Game. Parent behaviors are expressed as rate per minute of total commands, alpha commands, beta commands, warnings, questions, attends, and rewards. In addition, the percentage of parental attention contingent upon child compliance (i.e., rewards plus attends emitted within 5 seconds following child compliance) and the total number of TOs are computed. Child behaviors are expressed in percentages: percentage of child compliance to alpha commands, percentage of child compliance to total commands, and percentage of child inappropriate behavior.

Figure 2.4 shows a sample data sheet from the observation of the parent–child interactions during the Parent's Game in the clinic. The data from the sample observation are summarized at the bottom of the table. As can be seen, the child engaged in inappropriate behavior (e.g., whining, crying, hitting) in 40% of the 10 observation intervals of 30 seconds. The compliance to the total number of commands given by the parent was 19%. However, the compliance

FIG. 2.4. SAMPLE DATA SHEET FOR PARENT'S GAME

SCORE SHEET

Child's Name __Begood,__ _____ __Jack__ _____
_____ Last _____ First
Date __9/17/81__ _____ Time __5:30__ _____
Coder's Name ___JKL___ _____
Session ___/___ _____ Place ___Clinic___ _____

1

C	C	A	C	C				
			N	C				

(O)

2

A	A	C	C	Q	C			
					C			

(O)

3

C	C	Q	Q	C	C			
					C			

(✔)

4

R	C	C	C	Q				
			N					

(✔)

5

C	C	Q	A	C	C			
	C							

(O)

6

C	C	Q	C	C	C			

(✔)

7

A	A	R	C	C				
			C					

(O)

8

C	C	C	Q	W				

(O)

9

Q	A	Q	C	C				
			C					
			R					

(O)

10

C	C	Q	Q					

(✔)

ROW 1	ROW 2	ROW 3	CIRCLE	OTHER
C command	C compliance	A attend	✔ inappropriate	TO time-out
W warning	N noncompliance	R reward	child beh.	
Q question			O appropriate	
A attend			child beh.	
R reward				

32/5	=	6.4 Total commands/min.	11/5 = 2.2 Quest./min.	6/8 = 75% Compliance to alpha commands
8/5	=	1.6 Alpha commands/min.	7/5 = 1.4 Attends/min.	6/32 = 19% Compliance to total commands
24/5	=	4.8 Beta commands/min.	3/5 = .6 Rewards/min.	1/6 = 17% Contingent attention
1/5	=	.2 Warnings/min.		4/10 = 40% Inappropriate child behavior

to clear, direct commands (alpha commands) was much higher (75%). The parent provided positive consequences to only 16% of the child's compliances. Differentiating between child compliance to alpha and total commands provides the therapist with information concerning the antecedent events maintaining child noncompliance. In this example, the large difference between the percentages of compliance to alpha and total commands indicates that modification of the parent's command behavior is essential to treatment success. Based on this observation, the treatment goals would be the following: (1) to teach the parent to give alpha commands, (2) to decrease the number of beta commands, (3) to increase the parent's positive consequation of child compliance, and (4) to decrease the child's inappropriate behavior by teaching the parent a TO procedure.

Home Observations

Extensive data are collected in the home. An independent observer visits each home at a time convenient for the parent. This time is typically one in which the parent reports the problem behaviors to occur frequently. The time for the first observation is arranged near the end of the assessment (interview) session. The home observer is introduced to the parent and a mutually agreed-upon time is arranged. After the first observation, the parent and observer arrange the subsequent observation times. Sets of four observations occur prior to treatment, after treatment, and at follow-up assessments. Each observation is 40 minutes in length. Reliability data are obtained for 25% of the home observations by having two observers score the parent–child interactions.

For each observation, the parent is asked to interact with the child as would be normal in that situation. A number of procedural guidelines have been formulated in an attempt to facilitate the collection of data in the home. The parent is given a written handout describing these guidelines (see Figure 2.5), and the therapist discusses these with the parent near the end of the initial session.

As our coding system only permits the behavior of a single adult to be recorded at a time, observations have typically occurred with just one parent present. However, if it is possible for both parents to participate in observations, one parent's behavior with the child can be coded for 5 minutes and then the second parent's behavior can be coded for the next 5 minutes. This process can occur for 40 minutes, so that 20 minutes of data are collected for each parent. Alternatively, separate observation periods of 20 to 40 minutes may occur with each parent and the child.

Upon introducing the concept of home observations to the parent, it is frequently necessary to deal with the parent's reservations about home observations. The primary issue raised by most parents is the difficulty with following a normal routine when an observer is present. The parent should be assured that it is recognized that the observer's presence and the guidelines set up for the observation are not natural. However, these procedures are at present the most effective method available for obtaining information in the home environment. Parental concerns can be minimized by stressing that the information obtained will be used to design an effective treatment program for the child. Finally, the parent can be told that most parents report a habituation effect in which they become progressively less aware of and anxious about the observer's presence with each observation.

Data from each set of home observations are summarized in a manner similar to that for the clinic observation data. Figure 2.6 presents an Observation Data Summary Sheet for this purpose.

It is important to note that home observations are an expensive undertaking as extensive time and transportation costs are involved. While we value such an assessment procedure, we recognize that home observations may not be possible in many settings. Therefore, it is important to note again that our assessments in the clinic and in the home have yielded similar results (Peed et al., 1977). In addition, data collected in the home by parents have been shown to correlate with home observational data (Patterson & Fleischman, 1979). As a consequence, data collected during clinic

FIG. 2.5. PARENT'S GUIDELINES FOR HOME OBSERVATIONS

As we discussed during our initial meeting, allowing us to see you and your child in a more normal routine will help us to better design treatment and to determine its effectiveness. We appreciate you allowing us into your home.

When the observer arrives, you will see that he or she has a tape recorder and earphone. The observer is *not* recording the observation. The observer is listening to a tape that is cueing him or her when to code information. If you'd like, the observer can let you hear a portion of the tape.

Occasionally, two observers will come to your home. The second observer is there to check the recording accuracy of the first observer, *not* to evaluate your performance.

Concerning each observation: please try to interact normally with your child. Don't feel compelled to do anything you wouldn't ordinarily be doing at this time. Ignore the observer — he or she will try to be as unobtrusive as possible. During the observation, the observer will not be able to interact with you or your child.

It is very important that you follow these guidelines as closely as possible for each home observation. They are designed to help the observer hear and see as much of the observation as he or she can.

1. Remain in a two-room area with your child, in view and hearing range of the observer. If your child leaves the observation area, please bring the child back.

---

observations by an observer or therapist and in the home by a parent can serve as an adequate replacement for home observational data.

Observer Training

As noted earlier, training observers in the reliable use of a complex coding system is a difficult and time-consuming task. In this section, we describe briefly some of the procedures we use.

Our observers typically are undergraduate psychology majors who are selected as observers because of their interest in child psy-

FIG. 2.5. *continued*

2. You may bring any work materials or toys desired into the observation area, with the exception of commercial board games (e.g., Candyland, Monopoly, etc.) or playing cards. It is a good idea to do this *before* the observation starts. Also, we have found it helpful if you check on your child's bathroom needs prior to the beginning of the observation.

3. Do not watch tv.

4. Please don't read to your child.

5. It is best if your child not have friends over during the observation. If brothers or sisters are present, then they should be at the other observations as much as possible.

6. If the telephone rings, talk as briefly as possible, or ask if you may return the call later.

7. If you have any questions regarding your appointments at the clinic or concerning the treatment program, please do not ask the observer. Observers are not trained in these matters. If you will call us at the clinic, we will try to answer your concerns.

Don't be surprised if you feel a bit awkward at first — everyone does. However, if you just pretend the observer is not there, then you will be more comfortable and will act more naturally. Thank you for your cooperation.

---

chology. We attempt to select individuals who are highly motivated and are seeking a relevant field experience. The observers typically receive course credit in the form of an independent study course for their participation.

Observers are trained in groups of four or five. Initially, they are instructed to read the coding manual (Appendix B). The general framework within which the coding is done, the setting in which behavior is coded, and the individual behavior categories are then discussed. Subsequently, each behavior category and its general coding procedure is presented. Actual training then is initiated. One behavior at a time is taught. A behavior is selected; the

FIG. 2.6. OBSERVATION DATA SUMMARY SHEET

Child's Name _____

Observer's Name _____

Data Tallied By _____

Date of Observation _____

Condition: Pre, Post, or Follow-up

Behaviors

	1	2	3	4	Total
			Observations		
Row 1					
Attends	___	___	___	___	= (a) ___
Rewards	___	___	___	___	= (b) ___
Questions	___	___	___	___	= (c) ___
Warnings	___	___	___	___	= (d) ___
Total commands	___	___	___	___	= (e) ___
Beta commands	___	___	___	___	= (f) ___
Alpha commands	___	___	___	___	= (g) ___
Row 2					
Compliances to commands	___	___	___	___	= (h) ___
Compliances to warnings	___	___	___	___	= (i) ___
Noncompliances to commands	___	___	___	___	= (j) ___
Noncompliances to warnings	___	___	___	___	= (k) ___
Row 3					
Attends	___	___	___	___	= (l) ___
Rewards	___	___	___	___	= (m) ___

Other

Time-outs (TO) _____ _____ = (n)

Inappropriate behavior _____ _____ = (p)

(a + l) _____	÷ 160		_____	Attends per minute (p.m.)
(b + m) _____	÷ 160		_____	Rewards p.m.
(a + l + b + m) _____	÷ 160		_____	Attends + rewards p.m.
(c) _____	÷ 160		_____	Questions p.m.
(d) _____	÷ 160		_____	Warnings p.m.
(e) _____	÷ 160		_____	Total commands p.m.
(f) _____	÷ 160		_____	Beta commands p.m.
(g) _____	÷ 160		_____	Alpha commands p.m.
(h) _____	÷ (g)	× 100 =	_____	% Compliance to alpha commands
(h) _____	÷ (e)	× 100 =	_____	% Compliance to total commands
(j) _____	÷ (e)	× 100 =	_____	% Noncompliance to total commands
(i) _____	÷ (d)	× 100 =	_____	% Compliance to warnings
(k) _____	÷ (d)	× 100 =	_____	% Noncompliance to warnings
(l + m) _____	÷ (h + i)	× 100 =	_____	% Contingent attention
(p) _____	÷ 320		_____	% Intervals inappropriate behavior
			(n)	# Time-outs

definition is presented; the trainer models several examples of the behavior; and observers, enacting the parts of parent and child, take turns role-playing the behaviors with available toys while the remaining observers code the occurrence of the behavior being taught. Following each role play, the trainer and observers compare their recorded frequency of occurrence of the behavior. Agreements and disagreements are discussed.

After one behavior has been taught, a second behavior is then similarly taught. Subsequently, role playing occurs in which both behaviors are modeled and recorded by observers. In addition, written exercises are used to provide the observers with exposure to making various subtle discriminations (e.g., between a question and a question command). Each new behavior is taught in this manner. New behaviors are continually taught until observers can code all behaviors simultaneously in the role-played vignettes.

From this point on, training occurs primarily through the use of videotaped interactions. These may be tapes of simulated parent–child interactions employing the trainers or of actual parent–child interactions. The advantage of the former is that specific discriminations or types of interactions may be presented. The tapes of actual parent–child interactions provide a more realistic approximation to what the observer will experience in the home setting and are employed more frequently in the later stages of training.

Training continues until the observers have attained an acceptable level of skill in using the coding system. We have operationally defined this level as that of obtaining a reliability coefficient of 80% on a prescored 10-minute videotape of an actual parent–child interaction. The reliability coefficient for any one behavior is calculated by first computing the number of agreements between a prescored protocol and the trainee and the number of agreements plus disagreements for each 30-second interval. Each of these figures is summed across 30-second intervals and the total number of agreements between the trainee and the protocol is divided by the total number of agreements plus disagreements to obtain a reliability coefficient. It typically takes 20 to 25 hours of training for observers to reach this level of skill.

Training sessions occur two or three times weekly and each lasts 1 to 1½ hours. In the initial stages of training, sessions occur more frequently than they do in later stages. This is done in order to provide a more intensive exposure to the coding system early in the training sequence. Once observers are trained and are doing observations, group practice sessions are held weekly in order to insure that reliable scoring continues and to prevent observer drift.

Prior to their first home observation, observers are instructed in appropriate professional behavior. The importance of being prompt for observations is noted. While the observers are instructed to be courteous and polite at all times, they are requested not to socialize with parents. The confidentiality of the information gathered during the observations is stressed. Parental questions regarding treatment or child problems are to be referred to the therapist. Under no circumstances are observers to give advice or suggestions on how to manage children.

For their first home observation, observers are accompanied by an experienced observer. We have found that this minimizes much of the anticipatory anxiety the new observer may have and provides a model of appropriate professional behavior. In these situations, reliability data are collected as well. (Reliability checks are usually conducted during one of the later observation sessions to allow the parent to habituate to the primary observer's presence.)

3

TREATMENT

IN THIS CHAPTER, *we first present an overview of the parent training model and of our training program. This is followed by a description of the rationale for using the program to treat child noncompliance. Finally, Phase I and Phase II of the program are presented in detail.*

AN OVERVIEW

As noted in Chapter 1, we hypothesize that the child's noncompliant, deviant behavior is shaped and maintained through maladaptive patterns of family interaction, which reinforce coercive behaviors. As a logical outgrowth of this formulation, our treatment strategy involves teaching the parents to change their behavior toward the problem child so as to incorporate more appropriate styles of family interaction. Berkowitz and Graziano (1972) have noted several reasons for employing parents as mediators in such cases. First, since most of the child's coercive behavior is acquired and maintained in the natural environment (i.e., within the family), it is unlikely that clinically significant changes can be obtained by treating the child "out of context." Second, even if improvements are achieved in the child's behavior in the clinic, these will most likely dissipate if the child is returned to the natural environment that produced the problems in the first place. Finally, parents have the greatest contact with the child and the greatest control over the child's environment and, by virtue of their parenthood, have the major moral, ethical, and legal responsibility to care for the child.

Most of the initial work aimed at reprogramming the social environment of children via training the parents was limited to descriptive case studies or single-case designs with data collected in the laboratory or home. One of the first attempts to teach parents to alter coercive child behavior was conducted by Williams in 1959. Since then, hundreds of parent training studies have appeared. Recent reviews of these investigations (Forehand, 1977; O'Dell, 1974; Wells & Forehand, 1981) indicate that training parents to change their children's behavior can be a highly effective intervention procedure.

It is important to note that parent training is not effective with all families. For example, Patterson (1974) reported that 22% of the treated families in his sample did not show improvement with parent training. Similarly, in our work an examination of individual subject data clearly indicates that some parents and children do not change on some of our outcome measures. Furthermore, as with other types of treatment for children, dropouts occur in parent training (McMahon, Forehand, Griest, & Wells, 1981; Patterson & Fleischman, 1979). Parent depression (McMahon, Forehand, Griest, & Wells, 1981), low socioeconomic status (McMahon, Forehand, Griest, & Wells, 1981; Patterson, 1974), and referral by authority sources in contrast to self-referral (Worland, Carney, Weinberg, & Milich, in press) are associated with poor therapy outcome and/or high dropout rates in parent training. Obviously, therapists should be sensitive to the potential effects of these variables when accepting clients into therapy. Although data are not yet available, Fleischman, Shilton, and Arthur (1979) have recently devel-

oped a scale to measure client readiness for parent behavioral training. Once such a scale is validated, it will be invaluable in assisting
the therapist in determining which families are ready for (and can
profit from) parent training.

Regardless of the limitations noted above, we have found
parent training to be the most effective approach available for
modifying child noncompliance in the home. Therefore, this
chapter and the following one consist of a detailed description of
our parent training program.

The Training Setting

Parent training has occurred either in the home or in the clinic.
Obviously, there are advantages and disadvantages to each approach. Training in the home prevents the need for generalization
from the clinic to the home to occur. However, home training
requires substantially more time and expense on the part of the
therapist (e.g., travel time and gas expenses). As noted earlier, our
program is based on a clinic training model as this appears to be
more efficient and, therefore, the most likely to be employed by
most mental health professionals. We have also spent substantial
time and effort in our research endeavors to examine and facilitate
generalization from the clinic to the natural environment (see
Chapter 6).

Treatment is initiated and carried out with individual families
(rather than in groups) in a clinic playroom similar to the one used
for clinic observations. The treatment room is equipped with a one-
way window and a bug-in-the-ear communication system (which
can be obtained from Farrall Instruments, P.O. Box 1037, Grand
Island, Nebraska 68801), giving the therapist the ability to unobtrusively talk to the parent while the parent interacts with the child.

Treatment sessions are optimally scheduled twice each week.
Because the program is so practice-oriented, we have found that
the more traditional format of weekly sessions resulted in an unac-

ceptable level of performance decay. If parents were having difficulty implementing a procedure at home, they tended either to stop using the skill, or worse, to become quite proficient at using it incorrectly. By attending two sessions each week, parents receive a more constant level of feedback and training. When practical considerations (e.g., distance) prevent twice-weekly sessions, it is strongly recommended that phone contact occur midway between sessions.

Therapists

We have typically employed two therapists to work with each family. This has a dual purpose. First, it enables the therapists to be more flexible in demonstrating various skills to the parent. In the initial stages of teaching a new skill, one therapist models the skill while the other therapist role-plays the child. This allows the parent to devote full attention to the modeling of the parenting skill. A second advantage of employing cotherapists is that it permits students or others who are inexperienced with the program to learn from *in vivo* exposure. As the student becomes more experienced and comfortable in the role of cotherapist, he or she assumes a greater proportion of the teaching role. Eventually, this person may function as a primary therapist. However, this is obviously an expensive procedure in terms of personnel, and whether it is appropriate in a particular setting will need to be determined for each individual case. It is certainly possible for a single therapist to conduct the parenting program.

Clinical Skills

Little behavioral research is available to suggest which general clinical skills are necessary for therapists who engage in behavioral parent training. In the only available study, Alexander, Barton, Schiavo, and Parsons (1976) reported that therapists' use of warmth and humor was critical for the treatment to be successful. Although we have not systematically defined and measured them, we believe that the therapist's warmth, humor, genuineness, and honesty are critical ingredients in our program. These skills are especially important in dealing with parents who initially are expecting another therapeutic approach, who may feel guilty, who may be shy or reserved in practicing the skills being taught, or who may view reinforcement as bribery. Guidelines for handling each of these issues are presented in Chapter 4. However, it is important to note here that an empathetic understanding of the parent's point of view is essential in handling situations such as these that arise in parent training.

Parenting Skills

A major issue in training parents to modify their children's behavior concerns the skills to be taught. Which skills can parents most effectively use to modify child noncompliance and other deviant behavior? Our research supports the teaching of five skills: giving attends, giving rewards, ignoring, issuing commands, and implementing TO. These parenting techniques are described in detail in this chapter and the following one, and Chapter 6 presents the data from studies examining these skills.

Our clinical experience has indicated that these skills need to be taught in a specific order. Primarily, it is important that the attending and rewarding skills be taught prior to the teaching of commands and TO. We have found that parents who are first taught a disciplinary procedure such as TO (which is a type of punishment) will frequently reduce their children's problem behaviors and terminate therapy. Unfortunately, these parents have not learned any positive skills for interacting with their children or for maintaining their children's positive behavior. Therefore, for both ethical reasons and overall therapeutic effectiveness, it is important to teach punishment procedures to parents last in the therapy process.

Method of Teaching

Another major issue in training parents to modify their children's behavior is how to teach the parents the skills they should learn. A therapist can simply instruct parents in what to do, give them a handout that describes the technique, model the skill, and/or have the parents role-play the skill. Recent research (Flanagan, Adams, & Forehand, 1979; Nay, 1975) indicates that modeling and role playing are the most effective teaching procedures in parent training. These findings basically confirm the model upon which our treatment program is based. Although we employ all of the teaching methods noted above, we place primary emphasis upon modeling and role playing. In addition, the parents are given homework assignments in which they employ the skill at home with their child. This model involves a gradual shaping procedure in which parents are told, are shown, practice, and generalize to the home each new skill.

Overview of the Treatment Program

The treatment program itself consists of two phases. During the differential attention phase of treatment (Phase I), the parent is taught to be a more effective reinforcing agent. In the context of the Child's Game, the parent is trained to increase the frequency and range of social rewards and eliminate verbal behaviors — commands, questions, and criticisms (Forehand & Scarboro, 1975; Johnson & Lobitz, 1974b) — that are associated with deviant child behavior. First, the parent is taught to attend to and describe the child's appropriate behavior. Moreover, the parent is required to eliminate all commands, questions, and criticisms directed to the child during the clinic training session. The second segment of Phase I consists of training the parent in the use of rewards contingent upon compliance and other appropriate behaviors. In particular, the parent is taught to use praise statements in which the child's desirable behavior is labeled (e.g., "You are a good boy for picking up the blocks"). Throughout Phase I, the therapist emphasizes the use of contingent attention to increase child behaviors that the parent considers desirable. Furthermore, the parent is taught to ignore minor inappropriate behaviors. In the home, the parent is required to structure daily 10- to 15-minute Child's Games to practice the skills that were learned in the clinic. With the aid of the therapist, the parent formulates lists of child behaviors that he or she wishes to increase. The contingent use of attends and rewards to increase these behaviors is also discussed. The parent is required to develop programs for use outside of the clinic to increase at least two child behaviors using the new skills.

The second phase of the treatment program (Phase II) consists of training the parent to use appropriate commands and TO to decrease noncompliant behavior exhibited by the child. The parent is trained in the context of the Parent's Game to give direct, single commands and to allow the child 5 seconds to initiate compliance. If compliance is initiated within 5 seconds of the command, the parent is taught to reward or attend to the child within 5 seconds of the compliance initiation. If compliance is not initiated, the parent is trained to use a TO procedure involving the following event sequence. A warning is given that labels the TO consequence for continued noncompliance (e.g., "If you do not _____, you will have to sit in the chair in the corner"). If compliance does not occur within 5 seconds following the warning, the child is placed in a chair in the corner of the room. The child must remain in the chair for 3 minutes and be quiet and still for the last 15 seconds. The child is then returned to the uncompleted task and given the initial command. Compliance is followed by contingent attention from the parent. In practice with the child during Parent's Game in the clinic, the parent is instructed to give a series of appropriate commands and to provide appropriate consequences for compliance and noncompliance. In the home, the parent practices the use of appropriate commands, positive consequences for compliance, and, finally, the use of the TO procedure for noncompliance.

Content of Sessions

The number of treatment sessions necessary for the completion of each phase of treatment depends upon the speed with which the parent demonstrates competence in the skills being taught and the child's response to this intervention. The number of treatment sessions for each client necessary for the completion of the entire treatment program has ranged between 5 and 12 sessions. The mean number has been approximately 9 treatment sessions. Each session is 60 to 90 minutes in length and consists of the following activities:

1. A 5-minute data-gathering period in which the therapist observes the parent and child playing either Child's Game (Phase I) or Parent's Game (Phase II)
2. Discussion with the parent about the use of attends, rewards, ignoring, commands, or TO during the preceding observation period and at home (which is discussed depends on the skill being trained)
3. Modeling of additional attends, rewards, ignoring, commands, or TO techniques for the parent by the therapist
4. Practice of the techniques in a role-playing situation with the therapist acting the part of the child
5. Explanation of the procedures to the child at his or her level, having the child repeat the procedures verbally, and role-playing situations with the child
6. A practice period for the parent in either the Child's Game (Phase I) or the Parent's Game (Phase II), in which the parent wears a bug-in-the-ear and receives instructions and feedback from the therapist. (If a one-way observation window or bug-in-the-ear is not available, the therapist can sit in a corner of

the therapy room and provide nonverbal prompts and feedback—by way of sign cards or hand signals—to the parent.)
7. Additional practice for the parent with the child in the
clinic but without ongoing feedback from the therapist
8. Assignment of specific homework to practice the skills at
home

Treatment Criteria

Movement from one segment of treatment to another is determined by the use of behavioral and temporal (number of sessions)
criteria. The therapist uses the data collected during the first step
of each treatment session to determine if the parent-child pair has
attained the behavioral criteria necessary for movement to the next
segment of treatment. The behavioral criteria insure that the
parent has attained an acceptable degree of competence in a particular skill before being taught additional parenting techniques.
This is critical, since the parenting skills build on one another. In
addition, these criteria allow for the individualization of the treatment program by allocating training time more efficiently. Some
parents require more training in some parenting skills than in
others. The behavioral criteria allow a flexible approach whereby
the therapist can devote maximum attention to the more serious
deficiencies. The treatment criteria for each skill are presented in
later sections in this chapter.

Conclusions

The parent training program is highly standardized, with the parent proceeding through a set sequence of parenting skills taught in
a particular manner. Despite this standardization, the program is
also quite flexible. For example, the treatment criteria insure that
the parent will attain a certain level of proficiency in one parenting technique before moving to the next skill. In addition, they
make it more likely that training time will be allocated most effi-

ciently. Skills that are acquired more rapidly (i.e., the behavioral criteria are met early) will consume much less time than those skills with which the parent is having difficulty. It is also important to note that each parent and child "team" presents unique personalities, problems, and strengths. The steps necessary to convince one parent to try a particular procedure with a child may be quite different from those required to convince a second parent. Furthermore, some parents present intense personal problems that have to receive attention as part of the therapeutic process (see Chapter 4). Nevertheless, as long as the child's behavior is the primary difficulty, we have found it to be most effective to continue with the treatment program until it is completed, acknowledging and providing help where possible with the secondary problems. If necessary, the secondary problems can then be addressed.

RATIONALE

Once the assessment process is completed and it has been decided that the parent training program is the most appropriate form of intervention, then the first treatment session is scheduled. The primary tasks of the first session are to provide the parent with a conceptualization of the presenting problem(s) in the context of the parent-child interaction and to present the rationale of the parent training program. The therapist also uses the child's behavior during the first treatment session as a means of demonstrating the effectiveness of social learning procedures. Finally, training in Phase I of the program usually begins in the first session.

The conceptualization begins with the therapist briefly summarizing the situations in which noncompliance and related problem behaviors occur. The coercive nature of the parent-child interactions is noted and briefly explained. Once the conceptualization has been presented to and discussed with the parent, then the therapist formally begins the treatment program by presenting a rationale and general overview of the program. The rationale for the program basically involves informing the parent that much of a child's behavior is learned. As such, the best approach for changing the child's inappropriate behavior is to teach the child more acceptable behaviors. Since young children are most influenced by their parents, then the purpose of the training is to teach the parent effective ways to interact with the child.

The parent is then told that the treatment program is formulated to deal specifically with noncompliance. It is pointed out that noncompliance was indicated as a primary problem during the assessment process. Most child behavior problems can be viewed as a failure to comply to some command or rule that is in effect; therefore, they can also be successfully treated within this framework. At this point, the therapist draws the two bar graphs in Figure 3.1 for the parent. It is pointed out by the therapist that the child is engaging in an undesirably high amount of noncompliant or inappropriate behavior at present compared to a relatively low proportion of compliance or appropriate behavior. Pointing to the second histogram, the therapist notes that a more desirable goal is the situation in which the child engages in compliant or appropriate behavior most of the time. The therapist also points out that even in the most desirable of scenarios, there is still some amount of inappropriate or noncompliant behavior.

FIG. 3.1. HISTOGRAMS OF PRESENT AND DESIRED COMPLIANCE/ NONCOMPLIANCE RATIOS

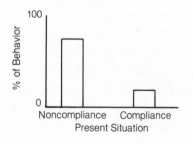 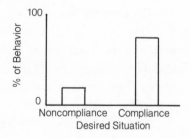

The therapist then describes the two major alternatives for reducing noncompliant behavior. The first approach focuses on the lowering of noncompliance directly. We tend to do this by punishment of one sort or another (spanking, loss of privileges, etc.). Unfortunately, while the particular noncompliant behavior may decrease in frequency temporarily, punishment does not necessarily increase the amount of compliance. This is because most types of punishment fail to provide an alternative appropriate behavior to take the place of the inappropriate behavior. In other words, punishment tells the child what not to do but does not teach the child an appropriate behavioral alternative. In this situation, the child may substitute a different inappropriate behavior for the punished response. It is also pointed out that if the initial focus is on reducing noncompliance by punishment, then the parent will have to punish the child frequently. Although punishment is necessary on certain occasions, excessive punishment is distressing for both the parent and the child and may cause guilt in the parent and anxiety in the child.

The therapist states that for these reasons greater progress can be made by focusing on increasing compliance. When compliance increases, then noncompliance automatically decreases! This is explained to the parent in the sense that the more time the child spends being good, the less time is available to be bad. The major advantage of this approach is that it lets the child know exactly what behavior he or she is to substitute for noncompliance. The parent is told that this focus remedies many child behavior problems and is a necessary first step in the treatment of all of them. A side benefit is that by decreasing noncompliance, punishment can be used much less frequently, but in a more effective manner. Finally, a focus on increasing child compliance makes for a much more pleasant family life, since the parent's positive influence on the child is increased and a positive parent–child relationship is facilitated.

A general overview of the treatment program is then provided. The overview begins with the statement that the program will help the parent learn both sets of skills (i.e., those for increasing compliance and those for decreasing noncompliance). The program is divided into two phases. In Phase I, the parent is taught specific ways to increase the child's good behavior. Phase I is considered to be the most important part of the program since it is critical for a positive parent–child relationship. In addition, this phase serves as the foundation upon which the effectiveness of the other parenting skills is based. In Phase II, the parent is taught how to deal with noncompliance directly. The parent is instructed in how to give clear directions to the child and how to provide appropriate consequences for the child's compliance or noncompliance to these commands. Finally, the need for consistency in dealing with the child is emphasized. Consistency provides a more secure environment for the child and one in which he or she will have to test limits less frequently.

Once the overview of the program has been presented and the parent's questions answered, the therapist then describes the mechanics of the treatment program. The therapist first stresses that this is an active treatment program with the parent serving as the primary agent in changing the child's behavior. The importance of the parent–child interaction in changing the child's behavior is reiterated. The parent is then told that he or she will be learning a number of parenting skills that have been shown to be highly effective in interacting with children and improving their behavior. The training format for each skill is then described in the following way. The parent is told that he or she will proceed through each technique or set of techniques in a number of small steps in the clinic. It is explained that this procedure is used to maximize the parent's learning and to make the parent feel more comfortable. The parent is then told that the following procedures will be used in teaching each skill:

1. The procedure and rationale for each skill will be explained.
2. The therapist will demonstrate the skill via role playing.

3. The parent will then practice the skill with the therapist role-playing the child.

4. An explanation of the procedure will be given to the child. The child will repeat the procedure verbally and will participate in role plays of situations involving the procedure.

5. The parent will practice with the child in the clinic. The therapist will observe and coach from behind the one-way window with the bug-in-the-ear. (The device should be demonstrated to the parent.)

6. The parent will practice with the child in the clinic but without the bug-in-the-ear device.

7. Specific homework will be assigned to practice the skills at home.

The parent is then told that the program is geared to the individual's own rate of progress. The parent is assured that training in a particular skill will continue until he or she is comfortable with that technique and has met a set performance criterion found to be necessary if the parenting skills are to be used for maximum benefit. Brief 5-minute observations at the beginning of each session and at other times will be used to assess not only the performance criteria for each skill but also to provide important behavioral data for discussion.

Finally, the first treatment session usually presents an opportunity for demonstrating the effectiveness of social learning procedures to the parent. We typically have the child present in the therapy room with the parent throughout the program while the therapist and parent are discussing and practicing the parenting skills. It is an excellent opportunity to demonstrate the relevant skills to the parent and demonstrate how quickly they can be effective. It seems that a stranger (in this case, the therapist) is often able to elicit appropriate behavior from children more readily than their parents can. In fact, data from several studies (Landauer, Carlsmith, & Lepper, 1970; Rudestam, Fisher, & Fiester, 1974) indicate that children are more compliant to strangers than to parents. The therapist can make use of this phenomenon by demonstrating the appropriate parenting skills within the session with the child. This is most beneficial in the first treatment sessions, when the parent is likely to be a bit skeptical that social learning techniques can be effective with the child. By seeing them successfully employed in a "real life" situation, probably quite similar to one experienced at home, the parent can be persuaded of the efficacy of the procedures early on.

At the beginning of the first treatment session, the therapist models an appropriate setting instruction to the child for the parent. The therapist tells the child, "[Name], your Mom and I are going to be talking over here. Here are some toys for you to play with. We have lot of work to do, so please don't interrupt us. If you do, we will ignore you." (This setting instruction should be repeated at the beginning of all further sessions by the parent.) The therapist then returns to the parent and presents the rationale of the program. After a minute or two has elapsed, the therapist interrupts the presentation of the rationale and says to the parent, "Since [name] has been playing quietly, I am going to let him [or her] know we appreciate that." The therapist walks over to the child and praises by saying, "Thanks for playing by yourself over here. We like it when you do that." The therapist then returns to the parent and resumes the presentation. This procedure should be repeated at variable intervals throughout the session, but with the parent providing the reinforcement to the child. Since the relevant parenting skills have not been covered, at first the therapist should tell the parent exactly what to say and when to say it. As the parent becomes more proficient at this, he or she should be encouraged to interrupt the therapist at appropriate intervals to reinforce the child for appropriate behavior. When the parent does this correctly within the session, the therapist should reinforce this behavior. During Phase I, the parent is encouraged to apply this "interrupting" procedure in the home when alone with the child or when interacting with a spouse, a friend, and so forth.

At some point during the first session, the therapist and/or parent is likely to have occasion to ignore the child's inappropriate behavior as well. This behavior is most likely to take some form of attention-seeking, such as attempting to interrupt the therapist or parent. Quite often this occurs soon after the child has been reinforced for appropriate behavior. This is because the child has not yet determined the reinforcement contingencies for particular behaviors. The child only knows that he or she likes the attention from the adults and, therefore, seeks more. When this inappropriate attention-seeking behavior occurs, the therapist again instructs the parent in the appropriate response—in this case, ignoring. After the situation has been handled successfully, the therapist can then provide a rationale for the extinction procedure (if this has not already been done).

PHASE I: DIFFERENTIAL ATTENTION

The focus of Phase I is to make the parent skilled in the use of differential attention to the child's behavior in order to increase the child's appropriate behavior and to help the child learn which behaviors need to be decreased in frequency or eliminated. Differential attention is the "application of adult attention following the occurrence of a desired behavior and the removal of an adult's attention after an undesired behavior" (Sajwaj & Dillon, 1977, p. 303).

Phase I is formulated on two assumptions.[1] The first is the "positive reinforcement rule," which states that whatever behavior is reinforced immediately after it occurs is likely to occur in the future. This rule is very important in starting and maintaining appropriate child behavior. The second rule is the "attention rule." It states that a child will work for attention from others, especially parents. The attention can be either positive (e.g., praise) or

1. The authors are indebted to Thomas R. DuHamel for this formulation.

negative (e.g., criticism, scolding) in nature. If the child is not receiving positive attention, then that child will work to receive negative attention, which he or she considers to be more desirable than no attention at all. Therefore, the parent's attention serves as a very powerful reinforcer to the child and can be used to change behavior.

In Phase I, the parent's goal is to increase the frequency of the child's desirable behavior by using parental attention to the child in a contingent manner, that is, by providing positive attention after appropriate behavior and withholding that attention after inappropriate behavior. A necessary prerequisite, however, is that the parent be able to provide meaningful positive attention to the child. A major purpose of Phase I is to reorient the pattern of parent–child interactions from a negative to a more positive focus. By the time most parents and children seek assistance from a mental health professional, all parties concerned can see little or no positive aspects to the other's behavior. The parenting skills taught in Phase I will teach the parent to observe the child's behavior more closely. Surprisingly for many parents, they discover that their child already engages in a fair share of positive behaviors. The task of Phase I then becomes increasing the frequency of those positive behaviors. This aspect of the program may be brought home to the parent by describing the typical parental attitude toward positive child behavior as "let sleeping dogs lie" or "leave well enough alone." The parent does not want to disturb the child when he or she is behaving, since the parent believes that the child will then demand attention continually. We emphasize that a more appropriate maxim is "Catch your child being good" (Becker, 1971).

A side benefit of Phase I is that it helps the parent slow down, enjoy the child, and relate to the child on the child's level. As the parent shows interest in the child and his or her activities, the child begins to enjoy interactions with the parent and the parent's value as a source of reinforcement increases. In essence, time spent with each other becomes "quality" time.

Three parenting skills are taught in Phase I. These include two types of positive reinforcement skills (attends and rewards) and an extinction procedure (ignoring). They will be described more fully in the next section. It is important to note that the positive reinforcement skills include only social types of positive reinforcement. Although we do occasionally find it necessary to establish behavior management programs that employ material reinforcers (stars, tokens, money), we have found social reinforcement to be at least as effective and more versatile. Parents will not run out of social reinforcers, as may happen with material reinforcers. In addition, use of social reinforcers obviates the need for later transfer of training from material to social reinforcement. Finally, social reinforcers tend to be more effective in maintaining appropriate behavior.

The Phase I parenting skills are taught within the context of the Child's Game. As noted in Chapter 2, the Child's Game is essentially a free-play situation in which the parent is instructed to engage in any activity that the child chooses and to allow the child to determine the nature and rules of the interaction. The Child's Game is used not only in the clinic setting but is also employed as a homework assignment throughout Phase I. Its use in the latter context is described later in this chapter. When the Child's Game is being explained to the parent, the therapist should acknowledge the artificial nature of a play setting in the clinic. However, the therapist also should note that the clinic presents an excellent setting for the parent to acquire and practice the parenting skills. The parent should be assured that the actual problem behaviors that are of particular concern will also be addressed.

Parenting Skills

Attends

This procedure employs a verbal description of the child's activity (e.g., "You're putting all the toys into the cabinet"). Attends are essentially a running commentary on the child's activity and, as such, provide a more constant source of attention than rewards (i.e., praise statements), which tend to be more discrete. There are two basic types of attends: those that simply describe overt behavior ("You're stacking the blocks" or "Here comes the truck"), and ones that may be used to emphasize a desired prosocial behavior ("You're playing all by yourself" or "You are talking in a normal voice").

In order to attend properly, the parent must first be able to follow the child's behavior; that is, the parent must be interested enough in the child's activity to observe what the child is doing in a relatively sustained manner. An occasional glance from behind the evening paper is not really following! There are also certain types of verbal behavior that should not be intermixed with attends. First of all, the parent should eliminate questions or commands directed to the child. They interrupt and/or structure the child's activity. Furthermore, the parent should refrain from turning the Child's Game into a teaching session ("Tell me what color this block is"). When the purpose of a parent–child interaction is to increase the child's appropriate behavior, then it is best not to teach the child or test the child's knowledge. In a similar manner, the parent should not attempt to direct the child's play. Participation in the activity is certainly appropriate and may include cooperative or parallel play. However, during such play, the parent should be reminded to continue to attend to the child's activity as opposed to his or her own.

It is also important to stress that attending is to be used only to describe appropriate child behavior. Although this point seems obvious, many parents who are novices at attending inadvertently reinforce their children's inappropriate behavior by attending to it. We have heard more than one parent say to a child, "Now you're throwing the blocks against the wall," or some other comment on the child's inappropriate behavior.

As noted above, attends can be employed as a more or less

constant form of attention. In essence, the parent is equipped with a "volume control" to raise or lower the intensity and frequency of the reinforcement. Therefore, attending is especially helpful when the parent is attempting to establish a new behavior in the child's repertoire or to maintain continued compliance to an extended activity. For example, a problematic situation that is commonly reported by parents is the child's failure to pick up toys after use. Even if the child has made some initial effort toward this goal, parents often report that the task is rarely completed. Attending may be used to maintain such activity by providing it on a constant basis as the child picks up the toys. Once the extended compliance is well established, the parent fades the frequency of attending to a more intermittent schedule.

It is not unusual for a parent to feel uncomfortable at first in using attends with the child. This is understandable since the parent is not used to this style of interacting. This awkwardness rapidly diminishes as the parent practices the skill in a variety of situations. When the parent first begins to practice attending, he or she may emit a relatively high proportion of rewards. This is because such praise statements are more familiar to the parent than attends, and the parent feels more comfortable using them. The therapist should encourage the parent to focus on attends to the exclusion of rewards so that he or she will become more proficient at and comfortable with this style of interacting with the child. Later in Phase I, the parent will be taught how to combine attends and rewards in the most effective manner.

It is also not uncommon for the child to remark upon the parent's new style of interacting. This is typically along the lines of "You're talking funny" or "Why are you talking like that?" We instruct the parent to respond by saying, "I'm just interested in what you're doing," and to ignore repeated questions by the child. This response is usually sufficient for the child. Furthermore, once children become accustomed to being attended to, they enjoy it immensely. A child will often engage in a discrete behavior (e.g., putting a block on top of another) and then look expectantly at the parent to see what he or she will say. As noted earlier, children very quickly come to enjoy this improved mode of interaction. However, in the event that the child is continually questioning the parent about attending, the parent would do well to examine the style and quality of attending and modify it as necessary.

The behavioral criterion for the successful completion of the attending segment of Phase I is at least one 5-minute observation of Child's Game in which the parent obtains (1) an average of four or more attends per minute and (2) an average of .4 or fewer commands plus questions per minute. Training in the attending segment of Phase I is typically limited to no more than four treatment sessions.

Rewards

The second positive reinforcement skill concerns the use of praise and physical contact and is taught in the latter part of Phase I. We teach parents three types of rewards. "Physical rewards" include various kinds of physical affection, such as a hug, kiss, pat on the back, and the like. The second type of reward is an "unlabeled verbal reward." These rewards include praise statements that, while positive in evaluation, do not tell the child exactly which behavior is being reinforced. Examples of unlabeled verbal rewards are the following: "Terrific!," "I liked that," and "Very nice." While nearly all parents are accustomed to giving out these first two types of rewards, at least on an occasional basis, they rarely employ the third category of rewards. "Labeled verbal rewards" are praise statements that specifically describe the particular child behavior that the parent is reinforcing. Examples include "Thank you for picking up the toys" and "I really like it when you do what Mom says." The advantage of this type of reward is that it teaches the child exactly which of several ongoing behaviors is being specifically reinforced. For example, if a parent walked through a room in which the child was playing quietly and gave an unlabeled verbal reward such as "That's nice," the child might attribute that praise to the tower of blocks he or she has just built, the quiet play, or the interesting mural the child has just drawn on the new wallpaper (out of sight, of course). Thus, we strongly emphasize the use of labeled verbal rewards as a means of social reinforcement. As a teaching aid, it is helpful to instruct the parent to pair an unlabeled verbal reward with an appropriate attend. This insures the labeling of the child's behavior.

It is also necessary to teach the parent how to reward the child. We emphasize four general guidelines: (1) rewards should *immediately* follow desirable behavior; (2) rewards should be *specific;* (3) rewards should be used *consistently,* especially when the child is first learning a desirable behavior, such as compliance to parental commands; and (4) once the behavior is well established, the frequency of rewards can be reduced to a more intermittent administration. We also emphasize that the parent must be sincere in the expression of rewards and must also be sure that the reward she or he emits is one that is socially reinforcing to the child. A reward offered in either a diffident or overly enthusiastic manner will likely have the opposite intended results on the child's behavior. Likewise, a big hug and kiss for a 7-year-old boy in front of his peers may be the "kiss of death" in that context. Finally, we also stress that rewards are not intended to replace attends. Rather, the two skills are most effectively employed in conjunction with one another. We advise the parent that attending is a more versatile technique that can be applied in most situations and for longer periods of time, while rewards can be utilized best to selectively evaluate particular child behaviors in a positive manner.

The behavioral criterion for the successful completion of the reward segment of Phase I is at least one 5-minute observation of Child's Game in which the parent obtains an average of four rewards plus attends per minute. Of this sum, at least two rewards per minute are required. The parent must also use an average of .4

or fewer commands plus questions per minute. Training in the use of rewards is typically limited to no more than four sessions.

Ignoring

The third skill that is taught in Phase I is used to extinguish most types of inappropriate child behavior. The parent is told that ignoring is a major way to decrease the child's inappropriate behavior and is much easier to use than punishment. Behavior tends to decrease when it does not receive attention. Most parents readily accept the rationale for utilizing an extinction procedure with the child. However, they also frequently report that they have tried ignoring and it did not work. For this reason, we have devised a series of component skills that make up an effective extinction procedure. These are the following:

1. No eye contact or nonverbal cues. Unfortunately, often when a child is engaging in behaviors the parent would like to eliminate, it is very difficult to ignore the activity. The child may anger the parent, or may even be rather cute. Whatever the reason, parents often reinforce this inappropriate behavior inadvertently by a brief smile, a frown, or even a glance at the child. For this reason, we instruct the parent to turn at least 90° (and preferably 180°) away from the child. The child will then be less likely to notice any inadvertent facial responses that might reinforce inappropriate behavior.

2. No verbal contact. The parent is instructed to refrain from any verbal contact with the child while the child is engaging in the inappropriate behavior. This usually presents a problem to the parent in at least two forms. The first has to do with whether the parent should provide a rationale or explanation to the child for ignoring him or her. This is compounded by the frequent occurrence of the child asking the parent why he or she is being ignored. It is imperative that the parent not maintain *any* verbal contact with the child once the ignoring

procedure has started. The appropriate time to provide a rationale for ignoring is when the child is behaving appropriately. Verbal contact at any other time is simply reinforcing the child's inappropriate behavior. We usually have the parent explain the ignoring procedure to the child in the session after the therapist has modeled the procedure for the parent and the parent has role-played it with the therapist. The sophistication of the explanation varies depending upon the age of the child, but generally consists of a verbal statement, such as, "Billy, I am going to ignore you when you're bad. That means I am going to turn around and not say anything to you. As soon as you stop being bad, I will stop ignoring you." The parent then demonstrates the ignoring technique to the child.

3. No physical contact. The child will often attempt to initiate physical contact with the parent once the parent has started to ignore. The child may tug on the parent, attempt to sit in the parent's lap, or, in rare instances, become aggressive. It is a good idea to have the parent stand when ignoring the child. This prevents the occurrence of lap-sitting, and it also provides a discriminative cue to the child that the parent is ignoring as opposed to simply being engrossed in some other activity. We also tell parents that in more severe cases they may find it necessary to leave the room in order to avoid reinforcing the child's inappropriate behavior. This "TO procedure in reverse" is useful, but it does have a serious shortcoming: the parent may not be aware that the inappropriate behavior has ceased if she or he is in another room. Since it is important that ignoring be terminated concurrently with the cessation of the child's inappropriate behavior, this solution is not the most desirable one.

Ignoring is an extremely useful and effective procedure for decreasing inappropriate behavior. However, there are some situations in which ignoring should *not* be employed. Basically, whenever children's behavior is damaging or has the potential to damage themselves, others, or property, a more active intervention (e.g., TO) should be utilized.

Training in the use of ignoring is usually limited to no more than the equivalent of a single treatment session. Ignoring occasionally has to be taught simultaneously with, rather than after, attending or rewarding when a child is excessively disruptive in a session. We have not typically utilized a specified behavioral criterion for successful demonstration of ignoring; however, a recommended criterion would be one in which the parent successfully ignores 70% of the child's inappropriate behavior in at least one 5-minute observation of the Child's Game.

It is important to stress to the parent the importance of performing all of the Phase I skills consistently. They are most effective when the child is provided with a large number of learning experiences in which the parent juxtaposes ignoring for the child's inappropriate behavior with positive attention (attends, rewards) for appropriate behavior.

Homework Assignments

Child's Game

The major homework assignment during Phase I is the daily practice of the Child's Game. The parent is asked to conduct the Child's Game with the child once a day for 10 to 15 minutes. The primary purpose is to allow the parent to have repeated intensive practice in the use of the various Phase I skills. The idea is that once the parent has attained a degree of skill and confidence in employing the Phase I skills with the child in a positive setting at home, that parent will be better equipped to apply the same skills to more problematic situations as part of later homework assignments. The parent is asked to begin the Child's Game assignment as soon as attending has been practiced in the clinic setting (during the first or the second session). Thus, the earlier assignments only involve attends. Later, the parent is asked to incorporate rewards and ignoring into the practice sessions after they have been taught in the clinic. The parent is given the Parent Record Sheet (Child's Game), on which he or she is asked to record the time of day, activity, and child's response for each practice session (see Appendix C). This record sheet is brought to each therapy session and discussed with the therapist.

There is a second major advantage of the Child's Game exercise, which has been somewhat serendipitous. Parents have come to realize that this format is an excellent way to share "quality" time with their children. The high intensity of parental attention and interest that this exercise requires has ensured that children genuinely enjoy their "special time." This fact has served as a prompt for the parents to do their homework assignment, since the children are sure to remind the parents that the Child's Game is past due. Nearly all parents, but especially those who are single and/or working and who are not able to spend great quantities of time with their children, have found the Child's Game quite helpful. Not only can the parent be guaranteed a positive interaction with the child but the termination of the exercise also serves as a discriminative cue for the parent's own "private time," in which time can be spent with a spouse, reading the paper, relaxing, and so forth. For these reasons, we usually recommend that the parent continue the daily practice of the Child's Game into Phase II and even after the program has officially terminated. Finally, when there is more than one child in the family, it is advisable for the parent to conduct separate Child's Game sessions with each child. In this manner, each child is assured of individual time with the parent, and jealousy between the siblings can be minimized.

Specific Problem Behaviors

While rewards are being taught, the parent is asked to generate a list of three behaviors that he or she would like to see the child engage in more frequently and bring it to the following session. At this time, the therapist discusses the behaviors with the parent and assists in setting up programs for one or two of the child behaviors the parent wishes to increase. By making the assignment one of increasing positive child behaviors, the therapist gives the parent practice in conceptualizing behavioral goals as positive events. Examples of goals that are frequently cited by parents during this part of the program are having the child pick up toys, get dressed promptly in the morning, play quietly alone, interact appropriately with siblings or peers, or go to bed when requested. The programs involve the use of the differential attention techniques. The first program should be relatively straightforward and it generally requires a moderate degree of direction from the therapist. The parent is encouraged to assume more responsibility in designing subsequent programs for the other child behaviors using these skills. The parent is asked to keep a daily record of these programs and to bring it to each session. As the parent becomes more proficient at employing the Phase I skills in the natural environment, he or she is encouraged to apply them to other problematic child behaviors.

Thus, the parent moves from employing discrete parenting skills in the Child's Game in the clinic to using differential attention in the home as a means of dealing with specific problem behaviors and developing a more positive pattern of interaction with the child. Successful use of Phase I skills will reduce the frequency and intensity of child problem behaviors *plus* improve the parent–child relationship.

PHASE II: COMPLIANCE TRAINING

As noted earlier, the program utilizes two major approaches to handling deviant child behavior. The second phase of the program is directly concerned with decreasing child noncompliance to parental commands. We feel that the parenting skills learned in Phase I of the program, which are designed to increase appropriate child behavior, are extremely effective in improving the parent's relationship with the child. However, there are times when a direct approach to dealing with child noncompliance is needed. It is important to emphasize that these new skills do not replace the differential attention skills. Indeed, Phase II skills are effective only when used in combination with Phase I skills. The skills taught in the second phase of the program focus on parent behaviors to increase child compliance and decrease child noncompliance. Both antecedent (commands) and consequent (rewarding compliance, applying a disciplinary procedure for noncompliance) behaviors are included. These parenting skills are taught in the context of the Parent's Game. In contrast with the free-play activity of the Child's Game, in the Parent's Game the parent structures the activity by issuing commands and providing consequences for compliance and noncompliance. The Parent's Game is not practiced in the home setting, but only at the clinic. After the relevant skills are mastered in the clinic, they are employed in the home.

Parenting Skills

Commands

The focus of most parent training programs has been to modify the consequent events of child responding (Forehand, 1977). Antecedent events that might elicit deviant child behavior have been generally ignored. The analysis of such antecedent events is particularly relevant for child noncompliance. In this case, the antecedent event is the parental command. As is reported in Chapter 6, our work in both the laboratory (Roberts, McMahon, Forehand, & Humphreys, 1978) and in treatment outcome studies (Peed et al., 1977) has demonstrated the clinical importance of parental command behavior in influencing child compliance.

Several aspects of giving commands initially are emphasized to the parent. First, the importance of deciding ahead of time whether to give a command is stressed. Second, the parent is cautioned about giving commands in an indiscriminate manner (i.e., assuming an authoritarian style of interaction with the child). Third, the parent is told not to give a command unless she or he is prepared to ensure that compliance follows it, regardless of how long that may take.

The parent is then told that the focus of command training is to teach him or her to give clear, direct commands to the child. In this manner, the parent can have a powerful positive influence on the rate of child compliance. The moral and ethical responsibility of giving clear commands is stressed to the parent. If the child does not follow a parental command, the parent needs to be sure it is because the child chose to be noncompliant, not because of a failure to understand the directive.

A number of poor commands (beta commands) are then listed and described. There are five general types of commands that can lower the rate of child compliance, as follows:

1. Chain commands. These are a series of commands strung together, which may require the completion of several unrelated activities (e.g., "Pick up the blocks and put them in the box, then make your bed and put the dirty clothes in the hamper"). Depending upon the age of the child, chain commands may result in an information overload with a resultant failure of the child to comply. Even where this is not an issue, however, chain commands preclude a clear definition of compliance unless the child complies to all parts of the chain.

2. Vague commands. These directives do not specify observable behaviors to be performed by the child and, as such, present an ambiguous situation for the child. Classic vague commands include "Be careful," "Watch out," and "Be a good boy." Although the parent probably often has some specific behaviors in mind when issuing these commands (e.g., "Don't run into the street" or "Don't hit your brother"), the child has not acquired a long enough learning history to associate these vague directives with the specific behaviors. The consequence, at least from the parent's view, is noncompliance.

3. Question commands. These are perhaps the most problematic type of command for parents. At issue here is the subtle discrimination between a request and a command. A request implies that the receiver has the option of choosing whether to do as the requester has asked. Commands are directives in which the parent expects the child to follow through on the instruction. This is relatively straightforward. However, this discrimination is blurred in adult–adult interactions. Most commands and requests to adults are phrased in a question format (e.g., "Would you work this weekend?"). Parents then use the same type of phrasing with their children when they give a command. They are usually surprised that when they say to their 6-year-old, "Would you like to take your bath now?" he or she says no. It is important to stress that requests themselves are not inappropriate. Rather, it is when the parent expects compliance to a command but phrases it as a request that it becomes problematic.

4. "Let's . . . " commands. These are commands stated in such a fashion as to include the parent ("Let's pick up the toys"). If the parent intends to assist the child in the activity, then this is an appropriate form of instruction. However, parents often use this to trap the child into beginning an activity. The parent has no intention of becoming involved. The child feels tricked, and the typical result is an uncompleted task and another round of escalation in the coercive cycle.

5. Commands followed by a rationale or other verbalizations. A rationale for a parental command is quite appropriate, especially with older children. However, analogous to the case of ignoring, the rationale should precede the command. For example, the parent might say, "We're having company tonight and I'd like the house to look nice. Please put away the toys in your room." In contrast, when the parent provides the rationale *following* the command, she or he is inadvertently obscuring the actual directive and increasing the likelihood that the child will not comply. Some children also will play the "why game" after commands as a way of avoiding the issue (e.g., "Why do I have to pick up my toys, Mommy?"). It is not unusual for parents to get sidetracked when giving a rationale after a command and to completely forget the original command.

Once these beta commands are described, the therapist should then ask the parent if he or she engages in any of these. Most parents report using at least one type of beta command with some frequency. We usually mention our own difficulties with particular types of poor commands. (One of the authors is noted for his mastery of question commands.)

The major thrust of the command-training segment of the program is to teach the parent to give appropriate commands (alpha commands) to the child. These commands are characteristically:

1. Specific and direct. The parent should first get the child's attention. The parent should call the child's name and pause until eye contact is established. The voice should be firm (but not angry) and slightly louder than usual. This is to provide a discriminative cue to the child that a command, as opposed to a request or other type of verbalization, will follow. The command should be phrased as a "do" command rather than a "stop" command if at all possible, since the former tells the child what behavior is expected. ("Do" commands are also easier for the parent to provide appropriate consequences.) The parent should say exactly what is meant without excessive verbalization and the command should be phrased in language the child can understand. If appropriate, gestures may be used to explain the command (e.g., pointing to the cupboard in which the toy should be placed).

2. Given one at a time. The parent should only give one directive at a time. If there are several tasks that she or he desires to be completed, a separate command should be issued for each one.

3. Followed by a wait of 5 seconds. The parent should not issue additional directives or any other verbalizations until the child initiates compliance or until 5 seconds have passed. (The following sections describe what further steps to take.)

The behavioral criterion for successful completion of the command segment of Phase II is at least one 5-minute observation of the Parent's Game in which the parent gives (1) an average of two or more alpha commands per minute, and (2) no more than 25% of the number of total commands as beta commands. Command training is limited to a maximum of two sessions.

Reinforcing Compliance

If the child *initiates* compliance within 5 seconds after the command is given, the parent is instructed to employ the positive reinforcement skills learned in Phase I (attends and rewards). The emphasis on the initiation of compliance allows the parent to reinforce compliance frequently and immediately. As noted earlier, attends are particularly useful in maintaining compliance to a task that takes some time to complete (e.g., picking up a number of toys). Labeled verbal rewards are most appropriate for the initiation and completion of compliance.

Consequences for Noncompliance: The Time-Out (TO) Procedure

If the child does not initiate compliance to a parental command within 5 seconds, then the parent is taught to employ a TO procedure as a consequence for noncompliance. The parent is told that although punishment is not a preferred mode of interacting with a child, it is a necessary and appropriate action to take on some occasions. TO is represented as a more extreme form of ignoring in which the child is removed from all sources of positive reinforcement (especially parental attention) for noncompliance. It is described as a relatively simple, guilt-free method of discipline that is an effective substitute for other methods of parental discipline, such as criticizing, hitting, and yelling. It allows the parent to avoid responding to the child in anger; therefore, the parent will be able to use punishment more consistently and less frequently.

The TO procedure that we employ consists of a series of alternative steps. Which alternative is chosen depends upon the child's behavior at each particular point. This sequence is presented in a flowchart in Figure 3.2. We usually draw this diagram for the parent as we explain the procedure (it is also included in Parent Handout 7, Appendix C).

The sequence begins with the parent giving an alpha command. If the child has not begun to comply within 5 seconds, the parent issues a warning. The warning is an "If . . . then" statement that specifies the desired behavior and the consequences for noncompliance ("If you don't pick up the toys, then you will have to sit in the chair"). The warning essentially functions as a second command. The parent again allows 5 seconds for compliance to be initiated. If the child complies following the warning, the parent immediately praises or attends to the child. The sequence is then ended. If the child fails to initiate compliance within 5 seconds after the warning, then TO is carried out. By this time, the parent should realize that the child does not intend to obey the command.

The parent takes the child firmly by the hand and places the child on a chair facing toward a corner of the room. He or she then says, "Since you didn't _____, you have to sit in the chair until I say you can get up." This should be stated in a matter-of-fact voice that indicates that the parent is not pleased with the child's behavior. The parent should not provide a rationale or argue with the child while taking the child to TO or while the child is in TO. As in other situations, the time for explaining the TO procedure is when the child is behaving appropriately. (A modeling/explana-

FIG. 3.2. THE PARENTAL COMMAND-CONSEQUENCE PROCEDURE

tion procedure for teaching the child about TO is described below.) Furthermore, the parent should completely ignore any temper tantrums, shouting, protesting, or promises to behave by the child on the way to TO or during TO.

The child should remain in TO for 3 minutes. Release from TO is contingent on 15 seconds of sitting quietly on the chair. In this way, the parent avoids inadvertently reinforcing any acting-out behavior that might be occurring when the 3-minute mark is reached. Thus, 3 minutes is the minimum length of a TO interval. When the child has been quiet for the 15-second interval, the parent goes to the TO area, removes the child from the chair, and returns to the situation that elicited the noncompliant behavior. The parent then repeats the original command. This is essential to the success of the TO procedure. First of all, it prevents the child from using TO as a means of avoiding compliance. Some children would much rather sit in the corner for 3 minutes than take out the trash, clean up the kitchen, and the like. More importantly, this procedure insures that the child learns the compliance behavior that is expected in that particular situation. When administered in this fashion, TO is truly a learning experience for the child.

Once the original command is repeated, then the entire sequence of events leading to TO potentially may be repeated as well. The usual case is that the child complies immediately after the command or after the warning. In our experience with this TO procedure, we have seen the whole cycle repeated for a single command on only two occasions.

Once the basic TO procedure has been described to the parent, the parent is then instructed what to do if the child decides to leave TO while it is still in force. The child should be immediately returned to the chair. The first time this ever occurs, the parent states, "If you get off the chair again, I will spank you." This warning is only presented once; that is, the first time the child ever leaves the chair. It is not repeated in subsequent TO periods. If the child gets off the chair again, the parent returns the child to the TO area. She or he then administers two (and only two) spanks on the child's bottom with an open hand. The parent is never to use any other object. The child is placed back on the chair, and the parent says, "If you get off the chair again, I will spank you again." If the child again leaves the chair, the parent repeats the procedure.

While we basically are opposed to physical punishment, we have found a mild spanking to be the most feasible backup for the child leaving the TO chair. Of course, such a backup is not appropriate in all cases (e.g., it would not be suitable for parents with a history of child abuse or for parents who oppose the use of spanking). For these families (or for therapists who oppose the use of spanking), other backups for leaving TO may be used (see Chapter 4). However, we have generally found that very few spankings are necessary once the child realizes the parent intends to be consistent. There is no longer a need for the child to test Mom's or Dad's word. Therefore, spankings play a *very* minor role in the overall treatment program. In addition, we generally have placed a limit of no more than three occasions of spanking occurring in a therapy session. This limit is set to prevent a high rate of physical punishment from occurring. If three occasions of spanking have been administered in a session, the parent and therapist can then resort to another backup procedure (e.g., the parent can leave the room or can restrain the child in the TO chair).

After the TO procedure is explained and diagrammed, the therapist then walks the parent through the procedure and its variations. The parent then practices the sequence (including appropriate use of spanking) with the therapist acting as the child. (The parent should spank the therapist on the forearm as this allows the therapist to gauge the force the parent is putting into the spank.) Once the parent is proficient at implementing the various aspects of the procedure, then the teaching focus shifts to the child. Since the child has been in the room while the prior training has been occurring, he or she is likely to be somewhat familiar with the TO procedure already. However, to insure that this is the case, the therapist and parent provide formal instruction in the procedure for the child.

The steps parallel those employed in teaching the parent about TO. The TO procedure is explained step by step at a level appropriate to the child. The procedure is then demonstrated to the child with the therapist playing the part of the child and the parent administering the consequences. At each step, the therapist asks the child, "What's next?" If the child is correct, the child is praised and the actions are carried out. If the child answers incorrectly or does not know, the therapist again verbalizes the step and the parent carries it out. With older children, there are two further steps that may be carried out. The parent can implement the various alternatives of the TO procedure with the child in a role-play situation. The "pretend" nature of this practice is emphasized. With some children, the child also can assume the part of the parent, while the therapist acts as the child. In this manner, the child's understanding of the procedure is assessed. The parent should never play the role of the child in this aspect of the training. Some children take this as a sign that parents can be put in TO. It is important that the gravity of the TO procedure be stressed to the child. The TO procedure is not a game and is not to be used with adults, siblings, or friends.

This instructional process has several positive benefits for both parent and child. It seems to facilitate the learning process for the child, thus resulting in less need for the parent to issue warnings, use TO, spank, and so forth. It also assuages a remaining qualm the parent often has concerning the use of TO: that the child does not understand, or will not accept, the procedure.

The behavioral criterion for the successful completion of the consequences segment of Phase II is at least one 5-minute observation of Parent's Game in which (1) a 75% child compliance ratio (child compliance/total parental commands) is obtained, and (2) a 60% reward plus attend ratio (parental rewards plus attends issued within 5 seconds following compliance/child compliance) is obtained. Training in the consequences segment of Phase II is limited to no more than three sessions.

Homework Assignments

Practicing Good Commands and Reinforcing Compliance

The first assignment that is given concerning parental command behavior is asking the parent to monitor the types of commands that he or she gives to the child. The parent can simply keep a frequency count of the alpha commands and various types of beta commands that are given to the child. The purpose of this assignment is to make the parent more aware of how she or he issues directives to the child. Once the parent has begun to practice appropriate commands in the clinic, she or he should be asked to engage in this behavior at home as well. With respect to the home practice, the parent is advised to present the child with commands with which the child is likely to comply. This is to provide the parent and child with some early successes in compliance training and to reduce the likelihood of noncompliance. The therapist should emphasize the importance of reinforcing compliance by using rewards and attends. Since the parent has not been taught the TO sequence at this point, noncompliance could be a rather frustrating experience for the parent (for this reason, it is a good idea to initiate TO training as quickly as possible after the completion of command training). As a stopgap measure, the parent is instructed to ignore noncompliance or handle it as it normally would be handled. The parent is given the Parent Record Sheet (Phase II) on which to record each command that he or she gives to the child as well as the child's response and parental use of positive consequences (attends, rewards) for compliance (see Appendix C).

Time-Out

Because the TO procedure is relatively more complex than the other parenting procedures taught in the program, we want to increase the likelihood that when TO is implemented in the home, it will be successful. The parent is not assigned to use TO at home until its proper use in the clinic setting has been demonstrated and the child generally remains in the chair during TO in clinic practice sessions. In fact, the therapist specifically asks the parent to refrain from using TO at home.

Once the parent is proficient in employing TO in the clinic setting, the parent is encouraged to employ it at home. The first step is to select an appropriate TO area. The parent is advised to place a chair in a corner of a room or hall. There should be no entertaining items, such as TV, radio, toys, or windows in the vicinity. For this reason, the child's bedroom is usually not a good place for a TO area. The parent is then asked to select a single situation in which noncompliance frequently occurs for the first use of TO at home. The parent is reminded to issue an appropriate command, reinforce compliance, and employ the TO procedure if necessary. She or he is asked to record each administration of alpha commands and warnings, the child's response, and the use of parental consequences for compliance (rewards, attends) and noncompliance (TO) on the Parent Record Sheet (Phase II), which was received earlier.

As in the clinic, it is emphasized to the parent that in the home no more than three occasions of spanking should occur for a child leaving the TO chair. In addition to the backup procedures that were mentioned when discussing the number of spankings to be used in the clinic, the parent can utilize several backup or alternative procedures in the home. These are presented in Chapter 4, under "Problems in the Use of Time-Out."

It is quite beneficial to phone the parent in the interval between sessions after this assignment is made as a means of monitoring the use of TO and providing feedback and support when necessary. Depending upon the client, the phone calls may even occur on a daily basis. It is very important that the parent be successful in these early implementations of TO. If not successful, the parent may lose confidence in the procedure and/or parenting abilities, and the child may become more difficult to control. Once TO is used successfully in the one situation in the home, at the next session the parent is instructed to employ the TO sequence for all instances of noncompliance at home. The parent continues to monitor use of TO in the home on the Parent Record Sheet (Phase II), which is brought to each treatment session.

Parents report that use of the TO sequence seems to follow a relatively predictable pattern. When the procedure is first implemented at home, the parent is required to use TO itself a fair percentage of the time. There may even be a few instances of the child getting out of the chair before being permitted to leave. The child is testing the parent to see if the parent will be consistent in the use of TO. Once the child learns that TO can be expected to occur on a reliable basis following noncompliance, the next stage begins. During this period, there is an increase in the number of compliances to warnings but not to the initial commands. The child is still testing the parent. When TO does occur, the child stays in the chair for the 3-minute period and then complies immediately to the subsequent repetition of the original command. Finally, the child settles into a developmentally appropriate routine. He or she complies to most commands after they are stated initially and, if not, the child usually complies with the warning statement when it is given. Noncompliance still occurs but on a sporadic basis. The child has learned that he or she can expect consistent consequences for each act of compliance or noncompliance.

The Final Session

After the parent has met the treatment criteria for Phase II and has been successfully employing the TO sequence in the home, termination of the parent training program is appropriate. (In some cases, therapeutic contact may continue around other issues, such as parental depression or the marital relationship.) As in all therapeutic endeavors, the client should be given a general idea as to when the program may be terminated well ahead of the expected termination date. The final session provides both the parent and the therapist with an opportunity to "wrap things up."

The parent is likely to have several procedural questions concerning particular situations that have arisen (or that she or he anticipates arising). By this time, the parent is equipped with the requisite knowledge and skills for handling most instances of problematic child behavior. Throughout the final stages of the program and especially in the final session, the therapist should encourage the parent to apply the skills already learned to these situations and should reinforce the parent for appropriate use of the skills. In a sense, the therapist's task is more one of encouragement than instruction in the final session(s).

The therapist should emphasize that consistent use of the parenting procedures is the key to the ultimate success of the program. The child will engage in less limit-testing and more appropriate behavior as he or she comes to realize that the parent provides predictable and consistent consequences for both appropriate and inappropriate behaviors. While the program is not a panacea, it will make family life a more enjoyable and profitable experience for all concerned. It only requires that the parent continue to work at employing the newly acquired parenting skills.

Finally, the parent also should be encouraged to contact the therapist if further questions or concerns arise. Depending upon the situation, at the last session the therapist may decide to schedule follow-up telephone calls or clinic visits.

4
TREATMENT: FURTHER ELABORATION

In THIS CHAPTER, *we present a session-by-session example of the treatment program in an outline form. Reference is made in parentheses to earlier sections of the text where the material is discussed in detail. A detailed example of one treatment session also is presented. Finally, we discuss how to handle certain types of problem situations that may arise in using the program. It is important to note that the actual content of individual sessions and the length of the program itself will vary according to the progress of the particular parent.*

EXAMPLE TREATMENT PROGRAM OUTLINE

Session 1

I. Setting instruction to child by therapist (Chapter 3, "Rationale")
   A. Therapist reinforces appropriate child behavior.
   B. Therapist prompts parent to reinforce child throughout session.

    C. Therapist/parent ignore as required.

II. Conceptualization of presenting problem(s)

    A. Assessment information is employed (Chapter 2).

    B. Situations are summarized in which noncompliance and problem behaviors occur (Chapter 2, Figure 2.1).

    C. Coercive nature of parent–child interaction is examined (Chapter 1).

III. Rationale of program (Chapter 3, "Rationale")

    A. Behavior is learned and can be changed.

    B. Focus is on changing child noncompliance.

    C. Compliance/noncompliance histograms are drawn (Chapter 3, Figure 3.1) and explained.

    D. Two approaches to decreasing noncompliance are presented.

        1. Discipline following noncompliance.

        2. Compliance reinforced.

IV. Overview of program (Chapter 3, "Rationale")

    A. Program is divided into two phases.

        1. Phase I increases positive behavior.

        2. Phase II decreases noncompliance.

    B. Importance of consistency is stressed.

V. Mechanics of program (Chapter 3, "Rationale")

    A. Treatment program is active.

        1. Parent is primary agent in changing child behavior.

        2. Parent learns number of skills for interacting with child.

    B. Training format is described.

        1. Explain.

        2. Demonstrate.

        3. Role-play with parent.

        4. Explain procedures to child.

        5. Practice with child in clinic (therapist feedback).

        6. Practice with child in clinic (no therapist feedback).

        7. Assign homework.

    C. Treatment criteria determine rate of progress.

VI. Phase I (Chapter 3, "Phase I: Differential Attention")
  A. Purpose and overview are presented.
    1. Make parent skilled in use of attention to manage child's behavior.
    2. Explain two assumptions on which Phase I is based.
      a. Positive reinforcement rule.
      b. Attention rule.
    3. Discuss advantages of Phase I skills.
      a. Change interactions from negative to positive.
      b. Increase parent's reinforcement value.
  B. Parent Handout 1 is given (Appendix C).
  C. Attends are introduced.
    1. Define.
    2. Cite advantages.
    3. Discuss Child's Game.
    4. Model skill for 10 minutes (therapist).
      a. Cotherapist or parent plays part of child.
      b. Primary therapist gives feedback.
    5. Role-play attending (briefly) with therapist (parent).
VII. Homework is assigned
  A. Therapist assigns daily 10–15 minute homework in which parent is to practice attending during Child's Game.
  B. Therapist gives Parent Handout 2 and Parent Record Sheet (Child's Game) (Appendix C) for recording homework.

Session 2

I. Therapist observes parent and child interacting in Child's Game and counts attends, rewards, commands, and questions.
II. Parent gives setting instruction to child.
  A. Parent is reminded to reinforce child throughout session.

B. Parent is reminded to ignore undesirable behavior.
III. Therapist and parent discuss interaction.
IV. Therapist reviews attending.
V. Therapist models attending.
VI. Parent role-plays attending with therapist.
VII. Parent practices attending with child and receives prompts and feedback from therapist.
VIII. Parent and therapist discuss interaction.
IX. Parent continues to practice and record attending during Child's Game at home.

Session 3

I. Session 2 is repeated unless in initial observation of parent and child the parent meets treatment criteria for attends (Chapter 3, "Phase I: Differential Attention").
II. Session 2 is repeated with modifications.
   A. Discuss homework.
      1. Did parent practice daily?
      2. Did child respond to attending?
   B. Reduce time spent on reviewing attending and modeling skills.
   C. Increase time spent on parent practicing skill with child.
   D. Observe parent and child interaction in Child's Game at end of session to determine whether parent meets treatment criteria for attends.
   E. Instruct parent to continue to practice attending in Child's Game at home.

Session 4

I. Session 3 is repeated unless the parent meets treatment criteria for attending in either final observation of Session 3 or initial observation of Session 4.

II. Rewards are discussed if attending criteria are met.
   A. Using types of rewards
      1. Physical
      2. Unlabeled verbal
      3. Labeled verbal
   B. Learning to reward
      1. Immediately
      2. Specifically
      3. Consistently
      4. Intermittently once behavior is well established
   C. Employing attends in conjunction with rewards
III. Therapist models three types of rewards and intermixing of rewards and attends.
IV. Parent role-plays rewards and intermixing of rewards and attends.
V. Ignoring is discussed.[1]
   A. Decreasing significantly the child's inappropriate behavior is a goal.
   B. Learning to ignore requires the following.
      1. No eye contact or nonverbal cues
      2. No verbal contact
      3. No physical contact
VI. Therapist models ignoring undesirable behavior.
VII. Parent role-plays ignoring.
VIII. Parent practices rewarding and ignoring with the child and receives prompts and feedback from therapist.
IX. Parent and therapist discuss interaction.
X. Therapist observes parent and child in Child's Game and counts attends, rewards, commands, and questions to deter-

---

1. As noted in Chapter 3, it may be necessary to teach the ignoring skill earlier in the program if the child is engaging in moderate levels of inappropriate behavior in the therapy room. Since the ignoring procedure can be taught independently of the positive reinforcement skills, it may be taught out of sequence. Parent Handout 5 should be given when ignoring is taught.

mine whether parent meets treatment criteria for rewards (Chapter 3, "Phase I: Differential Attention").

XI. Homework is assigned.

    A. Therapist assigns daily 10–15 minute homework in which parent is to practice attending, rewarding, and ignoring during Child's Game.

    B. Therapist asks parent to bring in list of three child behaviors that parent would like to increase.

XII. Therapist gives Parent Handouts 3, 4, and 5 (Appendix C).

Session 5

    I. Therapist observes parent and child interacting in Child's Game and counts attends, rewards, commands, and questions to determine whether parent meets treatment criteria for rewards.

    II. Parent gives setting instruction to child.

    III. If criteria for rewards are not met, the following occurs.

    A. Discuss interaction.

    B. Discuss homework.

    C. Repeat Session 4.

        1. Reduce time spent on didactic presentation.

        2. Increase time spent on parent role-playing and practicing with child.

    IV. If criteria are met or were met in Session 4, schedule proceeds as follows.

    A. Discuss interaction.

    B. Discuss homework.

    C. Discuss ways to use attends and rewards at home to increase desirable behavior.

    D. Assist parent in setting up programs for one or two of the child behaviors parent wishes to increase.

        1. Programs involve using attends, rewards, and ignoring.

2. Therapist takes major responsibility for setting up first program.

3. If time allows and first program is not too complex, a second program is set up with parent taking major responsibility for setting it up.

4. Parent is to implement programs and continue with daily Child's Game sessions at home.

E. Parent practices Phase I skills with child in clinic.

Session 6

I. Therapist observes parent and child interacting in Child's Game and counts attends, rewards, commands, and questions to determine whether parent meets treatment criteria for rewards.

II. Parent gives setting instruction to child.

III. Assuming that criteria for rewards have been met in Session 5 or at the beginning of Session 6, the following are scheduled. (If not, continue to practice rewarding skills.)

A. Discuss interaction.

B. Discuss homework.

1. Daily Child's Game practice sessions

2. Program(s) for child behaviors

3. Program(s) modified if necessary

4. Parent program(s) continued

IV. Phase II of program is introduced (Chapter 3, "Phase II: Compliance Training").

A. Review the two approaches to decreasing inappropriate child behavior.

B. Use Phase II skills in conjunction with skills learned in Phase I.

C. Focus Phase II skills on parent behaviors to increase child compliance.

1. Antecedent behaviors: how to give commands

   2. Consequent behaviors
      a. Reinforcing compliance
      b. Applying a TO procedure to noncompliance
   D. Teach skills in context of Parent's Game.
   E. Give Parent Handout 6 (Appendix C).
V. Command training is introduced.
   A. Emphasize that how parents give commands to their children is important in determining whether or not the child will comply.
   B. Discuss types of poor commands (beta commands).
      1. Chain commands ("Pick up toys, straighten table, brush teeth, and go to bed.")
      2. Vague commands ("Be careful.")
      3. Question commands ("Would you like to pick up your toys?")
      4. "Let's . . . " commands ("Let's clean up the yard.")
      5. Commands followed by rationale or other verbalizations ("Please put your clothes away. We're having guests tonight, and your room is a mess.")
         a. Actual command is obscured.
         b. Rationale is fine as long as it precedes the command.
   C. Present qualities of good commands (alpha commands).
      1. Specific and direct
         a. Say exactly what you mean.
         b. Make eye contact and keep your child's attention.
         c. Use a firm voice.
         d. Use gestures to further explain the command.
         e. Use "do" commands rather than "stop" commands whenever possible.
      2. One at a time
      3. Followed by 5 seconds of quiet by parent in order to allow child time to initiate compliance
   D. Give a command only if you are willing to follow through with it.

VI. Consequences for compliance are introduced.
   A. Reinforce child with attends and rewards if child initiates compliance within 5 seconds of command.
   B. Reinforce child upon completion of compliance.
   C. Emphasize that labeled rewards are especially important.
VII. Therapist models beta and alpha commands.
VIII. Parent role-plays alpha commands.
IX. Parent practices alpha commands with child.
   A. Tell parent to issue commands to child and reinforce compliance but to ignore noncompliance at present time.
   B. Deliver prompts and feedback to parent.
X. Homework is assigned.
   A. Instruct parent to monitor and record frequency of alpha and beta commands.
   B. Present child with commands with which he or she is likely to comply.
      1. Compliance reinforced
      2. Noncompliance ignored
XI. Give Parent Record Sheet (Phase II) to record use of commands and reinforcement for compliance (Appendix C).

Session 7

I. Therapist observes parent and child interacting in Parent's Game and counts alpha and beta commands to determine whether parent meets treatment criteria for commands (Chapter 3, "Phase II: Compliance Training").
II. Parent gives setting instruction to child.
III. If criteria for commands are not met, the following is scheduled.
   A. Discuss interaction.
   B. Discuss homework (including Phase I programs for child behaviors).

C. Repeat commanding as covered in Session 6, focusing on role playing and practice with child.

IV. If criteria for commands are met, proceed as follows.

A. Discuss interaction.

B. Discuss homework (including Phase I programs for child behaviors).

C. Introduce consequences for noncompliance.

1. Warning

2. Reinforcement for compliance to warning

3. TO for noncompliance to warning

a. Child stays in TO chair.

b. Child leaves TO chair.

4. Return to original command situation

D. Draw diagram of parental command–consequence procedures (Chapter 3, Figure 3.2).

E. Model consequences for compliance and noncompliance (therapist).

F. Role-play consequences for compliance and noncompliance (parent).

V. Homework is presented.

A. Assign parent to continue practicing giving alpha commands with which child is likely to comply.

B. Parent should continue to do the following.

1. Reinforce compliance.

2. Ignore noncompliance.

Session 8

I. Parent gives setting instruction to child.

II. Parent role-plays the following skills with therapist and therapist discusses and models when necessary.

A. Alpha commands

B. Consequences for compliance

C. Consequences for noncompliance

III. Therapist provides instruction (by using verbal instruction, modeling, and role playing) to the child in the consequences for compliance and noncompliance.

IV. Parent practices alpha commands and consequences for compliance and noncompliance with child and receives prompts and feedback from therapist.

V. Practice period is discussed.

VI. Therapist observes parent and child interacting in Parent's Game and counts parental alpha and beta commands, child compliances and noncompliances, parental attends, rewards, warnings, contingent attention, and TO to determine whether parent meets treatment criteria for consequences segment of Phase II (Chapter 3, "Phase II: Compliance Training").

VII. Interaction is discussed.

VIII. Homework is assigned.

A. Parent is responsible for selecting TO area in home.

B. If parent can use procedures correctly in clinic and child remains in chair during TO, assign homework of selecting one noncompliant situation, using alpha commands, reinforcing compliance, and using TO (if necessary).

C. If parent cannot use procedures correctly or child will not remain in chair during TO, repeat homework assignment from Session 7.

IX. Parent Handout 7 is given and parent is asked to record alpha commands and warnings, consequences for compliance, and use of TO on Parent Record Sheet (Phase II).

Session 9

I. Therapist observes parent and child in Parent's Game and counts parental alpha and beta commands, child compliances and noncompliances, parental attends, rewards, warnings, contingent attention, and TO to determine whether parent meets treatment criteria for consequences segment of Phase II (Chapter 3, "Phase II: Compliance Training").

II. Parent gives setting instruction to child.

III. If treatment criteria for consequences segment of Phase II are not met or child will not remain in chair during TO, the following sequence is used.
   A. Discuss interaction.
   B. Discuss homework if it was assigned.
   C. Repeat Session 8.

IV. If criteria for consequences segment of Phase II are met and child will remain in chair during TO, proceed as follows.
   A. Discuss interaction.
   B. Discuss homework if it was assigned.
   C. Discuss use of TO in various situations and for various behaviors outside the home (see "Commonly Encountered Situations" in this chapter for examples).

Session 10

I. If criteria for consequences segment of Phase II are met,
   A. Therapist observes parent and child in Child's Game and counts number of attends, rewards, commands, and questions.
   B. Therapist observes parent and child in Parent's Game and counts parental alpha and beta commands, child compliances and noncompliances, parental attends, rewards, warnings, contingent attention, and TO.

II. Parent gives setting instruction to child.

III. Therapist discusses preceding interactions and homework.

IV. Therapist and parent discuss any problem behaviors that are continuing.

V. Consistency is emphasized as key to program.

      A. Child will not need to test limits as much if parent is consistent.

      B. If parent is consistent, number and intensity of problems will be reduced.

  VI. Although program is not a cure-all, it will make family interactions more positive and enjoyable.

 VII. Continued use of Phase I skills is emphasized.

VIII. Parent is encouraged to contact therapist if difficulties arise.

EXAMPLE SESSION

In order to provide a further description of treatment, a session occurring during Phase I for one family (Mrs. M and John) is presented. In prior sessions the mother had previously been taught attending, rewarding, and ignoring skills. The session initially consisted of a 5-minute assessment observation of Mrs. M and John engaging in whatever activity the child wished (Child's Game). During the observation, Mrs. M emitted 21 praise statements, 10 attending statements, 1 command, and no questions. Subsequent to the observation, Mrs. M instructed John to play with the toys by himself while she talked with the therapist. The therapist discussed Mrs. M's use of attending and praise statements during the immediately preceding observation. Mrs. M reported that she believed she had attended to or praised most of John's desirable behaviors. The therapist agreed and commended Mrs. M for her performance. At this point, Mrs. M went over to John, who was playing quietly with the toys at the end of the room. She attended to his play for about 5 seconds and then praised him for playing quietly and not interrupting her while she and the therapist were talking. She then returned to her seat. The therapist praised Mrs. M for remembering to reinforce John's appropriate behavior. Mrs. M repeated this "interrupting" procedure several additional times throughout the session.

Mrs. M then was asked about her use of reinforcement with John at home. She gave the therapist her Parent Record Sheet (Child's Game), which indicated that she and John had engaged in the Child's Game on a daily basis since the end of the last treatment session. Mrs. M reported using attending and praise statements frequently in other situations as well, and indicated that John appeared to be responsive to such statements, as his behavior was becoming less aversive to her. She also reported that she had been able to ignore most of John's whining and demanding attention. Mrs. M then was asked to suggest one of John's behaviors that she might increase by the use of attending and praise statements. Mrs. M indicated that she wanted to increase the length of time that John remained in his room and did not demand attention by asking for various items during a 1-hour rest and quiet-play period after lunch. Mrs. M was asked how she might accomplish such a goal by her use of attends, rewards, and ignoring. She replied that she could reinforce him for periods of time that he did not demand attention and remained quietly in his room. The therapist agreed and suggested that she tell John to rest or play quietly in his room for 5 minutes and, after he remained quietly in his room for 5 minutes, she should go and reinforce him. She was told initially to reinforce him for each 5-minute period that he emitted the desired behavior. She also was told that after 1 week she could lengthen the interval between reinforcing statements to approximately 10 minutes. She was informed that during subsequent weeks, she could continue to lengthen the time intervals between reinforcing statements but never to fade out her attention entirely for John resting or playing quietly during this hour of the day. During rest period she was to ignore any of John's attempts to gain attention and matter-of-factly return him to his room if he left it. Mrs. M agreed to the intervention strategy and planned to implement it the following day after fully explaining it to John.

The importance of Mrs. M's attention to John was reviewed next, and she was reminded to make her attention to John contingent on his emission of desirable behaviors and to ignore his undesirable behavior. Subsequently, Mrs. M was told that the therapist wanted her to practice her use of attends and rewards with John. She was given the bug-in-the-ear, the therapist left the room, and for approximately 10 minutes, Mrs. M and John played activities chosen by John. During this time, the therapist prompted Mrs. M by way of the bug-in-the-ear regarding which reinforcing statements she could use and when to use them. The therapist also verbally reinforced Mrs. M for the use of reinforcing statements that she emitted without being prompted by the therapist. Following the parent–child interaction, Mrs. M was praised for her performance by the therapist. She was encouraged again to ignore inappropriate behavior and to use attends and rewards for appropriate behavior during the daily practice of the Child's Game at home, during normal activities with John, and during the rest period after lunch.

COMMONLY ENCOUNTERED SITUATIONS

The treatment program as presented in this chapter and the preceding one is relatively straightforward. However, there are a number of situations that can interrupt the progression through the program or that deserve special mention. The purpose of this section is to present some of these situations and the solutions we have developed for dealing with them.

The Play-Therapy Parent

Occasionally, a parent will not want to be part of the therapy process but rather wants the therapist to treat only the child. This is the parent who would like to drop the child off for treatment at 4:00, have the child "fixed," and pick up him or her at 5:00. Our approach to this type of parent is to explain that we believe the problem is not the child's or the parent's but is in the parent–child interaction. Therefore, it is necessary for both parent and child to be a part of the therapy process. Furthermore, we point out to the parent that since the child is with the parent the majority of the time, the most efficient and effective procedure is to teach the parent how to deal with the problems that are occurring. Even if we could effect some change in the child in a 1-hour individual therapy session, it is doubtful that the improvement would generalize to the home situation, where all other aspects of the environment, such as the parent's behavior, remain the same. By working through the parent, it is possible to achieve a more durable and effective change in the child's behavior.

This approach typically is effective in convincing the parent of the need for involvement. If the parent still does not wish to participate in therapy, a play therapist is recommended.

The Guilty Parent

Throughout the program, emphasis is placed on the fact that much of a child's behavior is learned and that the parent can change the child's undesirable behavior. Some parents immediately assume that the child's problems are solely their responsibility. These parents frequently wish to focus on a series of unpleasant past interactions between the child and parent.

It is important to acknowledge and respond empathically to the parent's feelings of guilt concerning past interactions with the child. However, we do not make these feelings a focus of treatment. Instead, we respond in several ways. The parent is reassured that he or she is not to blame for the child's problems and is told that it is not possible to look back into the past and accurately identify the causes of the child's problems. Even if possible, this knowledge would be of minimal assistance in resolving current problems. Therefore, we tell the parent that we wish to focus on the present. We encourage the parent to not worry about the past but, starting now, to work with the therapist to make some changes that will improve the interaction between parent and child.

The Extremely Deviant Child

As discussed in Chapter 3, we believe it is important to teach positive parenting skills (attending and rewarding) before teaching a disciplinary procedure. However, we have had 2 cases out of more than 100 clients in which the child was so deviant that it was impossible for the parent to practice and use the positive skills with the child until the disruptive behavior was addressed directly. In these two cases, we taught attending and rewarding to the parent, but did not have the parent practice the skills with the child in the clinic. Instead, we immediately taught TO to the parent, and then had the parent use TO and rewarding in practice sessions in the clinic and at home. Once the child's disruptive behavior was reduced, we then had the parent go through attending and rewarding with the child until the criteria for accomplishment of these skills were reached. (The criteria are delineated in Chapter 3, "Phase I: Differential Attention.")

It is important to emphasize that we rarely have found it necessary to deviate from the typical sequence of the treatment program. Therefore, use of TO prior to achieving the criteria for positive parenting skills should be reserved for extreme cases of deviance.

The Shy Parent

Some parents have difficulty practicing the skills taught in the program in front of the therapist. This may occur in the role playing with the therapist or in the practice session with the child. These parents frequently state that they can effectively use the skills at home but that they are too shy to try them in front of the therapist.

Our approach is to inform the parent in the initial therapy session that practicing the skills in the session will be an important part of the therapy process. With this initial statement, most parents are able to engage in the skills when the time arrives. The parent also tends to feel less inhibited in the role play and practice activities after the therapist has been observed involved in them as well. Once the parent starts to engage in the role playing, we elicit personal feelings about the activity, note progress, and again offer support. Appropriate reinforcement from the therapist for progress is most effective in relieving the parent of any "performance anxiety."

Reinforcement As Bribery

This objection to the use of reinforcement procedures is occasionally raised by a concerned parent early in Phase I. Because our parent training program relies so heavily on social reinforcement (as opposed to material reinforcers such as food and money), this issue rarely arises. However, if a parent does express concern about "bribing" the child, it will be necessary for the therapist to clarify the difference between bribery and reinforcement.

A "bribe" is defined as something that is offered or given to someone to induce him or her to act dishonestly. In other words, bribery is a misuse of reinforcement, for we have stressed that the parent's positive reinforcement skills are employed contingent upon appropriate behavior on the part of the child. The basic distinction between positive reinforcement and bribery, then, is the purpose of these procedures. Reinforcement should be given to teach the child various appropriate behaviors. Bribery would occur only if the parent were using reinforcement to corrupt the child's behavior (Krumboltz & Krumboltz, 1972).

Attending and the Older Child

We view the first part of the program where the parent is taught to attend to the child's behavior as being very important in improving parent–child interactions. Within the therapy session practice time with the child, the parent is prompted and encouraged to use attends at an extremely high rate. This is done because we realize that the rate of attends is likely to be substantially lower in the natural environment; therefore, we have the parent overlearn the skill in the therapy session to ingrain the skills as much as possible. This high schedule of attends in the therapy session sometimes leads the child to ask the parent, "Why are you talking funny?" or demand, "Stop saying those silly things." With the younger child, a parental response of "I'm just interested in what you're doing" is usually sufficient to remedy the situation. The young child rapidly acclimates to this new way of interacting with the parent and appears to enjoy the high rate of parental attention. With an older child (7 or 8 years of age), it is often necessary to have the parent use more varied attends and/or reduce the rate of attends during the practice session. This has handled the problem in nearly all cases. Interestingly, the parents report that the older children do appear to enjoy the attends at home — perhaps because of their lower rate of occurrence.

The Flat-Affect Parent

Occasionally, a parent will meet the criteria for attends and rewards (see Chapter 3) with respect to frequency, but the statements will be uttered in a flat tone of voice. It is clearly evident that these types of attends and rewards are not reinforcing to the child. In this case, the therapist must teach the parent appropriate affect to use with the child. This is not an easy task as it is difficult to specify behaviorally exactly what proper affect is. Nevertheless, we have found that the most effective teaching procedure is the same one used to teach the other skills used in the program: didactic discussion of the skill, modeling by the therapist, role playing by the parent with the therapist, and practice with the child. The modeling is particularly important as it is easier to demonstrate flat affect and proper affect than it is to verbally describe them.

We have found that with flat-affect parents it is easiest to teach the attending skill first and then the use of proper affect. Trying to teach both at once is too complex for most of these parents.

The Afraid-to-Confront Parent

Some parents learn and use the attending and rewarding skills very well but do not wish to confront their child by issuing clear, direct commands and using TO following noncompliance. This parent issues few commands during the Parent's Game and accepts the child's every excuse for not complying. In these cases, it is necessary to discuss the need to set firm and consistent limits for the child. Furthermore, in practice sessions with the child it may be necessary to give the parent commands to issue to the child and to tell the parent exactly when and how to implement TO. Only with this type of structure will this parent ever learn to deal with the issue of exerting any control over the child.

This parent also tends to express concern over the Parent's Game as being unfair to the child. The parent may say that non-compliance to the commands used in the Parent's Game (e.g., "Put the red block on the green block") does not justify the use of TO. The therapist should acknowledge the artificiality of the Parent's Game while at the same time pointing out to the parent that the basic issue is one of noncompliance to the parent, regardless of the particular command. The therapist should also point out that the purpose of the Parent's Game is to provide the parent with an opportunity to learn how to elicit compliance and minimize noncompliance and for the child to learn their consequences as well. At the same time, the therapist should also agree that the parent would not likely issue a command or use TO in such a situation at home and should stress the importance of giving appropriate commands in that setting.

Problems in the Use of Time-Out

Our TO sequence is a very exact, well-specified one. This is done in order to encourage the use of the procedure in a consistent manner, which, it is hoped, will reduce any difficulties that may arise. Nevertheless, we have found a number of potentially problematic situations can develop when using TO.

Some children may learn to never comply to the parental command but only to the subsequent warning. These children realize that the parental command will be followed by a warning, and that negative consequences will occur only for noncompliance to the warning. For these children, it may be necessary to have the parents employ TO immediately following noncompliance to the command. This strategy should be implemented only after several weeks of using TO, since, as noted in Chapter 3, this phenomenon may be only temporary.

A second problem concerns the child who says "I will do it now" when the parent begins to take him or her to TO. It is critical that the parent follow through with TO at this point. If the parent does not, the child learns that he or she does not have to obey until TO is actually initiated, rather than complying to the initial command or warning.

A third problem is the child who continually "pushes limits" while in TO. This may be moving the chair backward away from the corner or kicking the wall. For these types of behaviors, the parent needs to simply state, "If you _____, you will be spanked." Only major behaviors that cannot be ignored should be treated in this manner. It is important that the parent ignore as many minor behaviors as possible since TO is intended to temporarily isolate the child from sources of positive reinforcement.

A related problem is the child who refuses to come out of TO when the TO period is over. This child is trying to control the situation by dictating when he or she will leave TO. The parent should say, "Since you did not come out when I told you to, you must stay in TO until I tell you that you may come out." Another 3-minute TO then occurs. If necessary, the parent keeps repeating the procedure until the child is willing to leave TO. Fortunately, most children quickly realize that their bid for control in this situation is not likely to succeed after an additional period of TO.

A problem that often accompanies the use of TO is the child telling the parent that "I am going to run away," "I hate you," "You are mean," or "You don't love me." The parent must ignore these types of comments since they are another attempt to control the situation by the child. If the parent does not respond to these verbalizations, they will quickly extinguish.

Another TO problem concerns the use of a spanking when the child leaves the TO chair. We occasionally have felt the need to justify spanking with parents, even though most have employed this procedure with their children in the past. We tell the parent that we generally oppose physical punishment but that with young children there is no other backup for leaving the corner that is as effective. We point out that if the parent is consistent in spanking the child for leaving the corner, the child will soon realize the consequences will occur every time and will no longer test limits by leaving the chair. In addition, by instructing the child about TO in the clinic setting (see Chapter 3, "Phase II: Compliance Training"), it is less likely that the child will engage in as much limit-testing.

Several alternatives to spanking are available and can be used if desired. With older children, we have found that many do respond to removal of a privilege that is to occur at a later time (e.g., "If you leave the chair, you will not get to watch television tonight") as an alternative to spanking. Therefore, for the older child, removal of a privilege may be an effective backup for leaving the chair. For the younger child, three feasible options exist. One is to briefly isolate the child in a room that is well lighted, free of danger, and absent of entertaining items. A second alternative for the parent is to physically restrain the child in the TO chair. A third option is to provide a "logical consequence," should one be available (e.g., removal of some naturally occurring positive event such as playing outside with friends) (Dreikurs, 1964).

The Compliant Child

A situation that occasionally arises is that a child who is noncompliant in the home (as determined by parent report, parent-recorded data, and home observations) is compliant in the therapy sessions. As a consequence, the parent cannot practice the TO procedure with the child. We typically have the parent issue a number of commands to the child in an attempt to induce noncompliance. If this approach fails, we have the parent role-play the TO situation extensively with the therapist. The parent is then instructed to use the procedure at home. This training approach does not allow the therapist to prompt and instruct the parent in the actual use of TO with the child; however, the therapist can receive detailed feedback from the parent over the phone or at the next therapy session concerning the effectiveness of the procedure. Modeling and role playing can then be utilized to assist the parent in working out problems that exist. If difficulties with TO continue to occur in the home, the therapist can make a home visit, observe the parent's use of TO, and assist the parent with the correct implementation of the procedure.

Failure to Complete Homework Assignments or Attend Sessions

Occasionally, the therapist is faced with a parent who has failed to complete a homework assignment or who misses appointments. A single occurrence is not considered significant; however, repeated failure to complete the assignments or missed appointments should be a danger signal to the therapist. The therapist should attempt to determine if there are environmental factors that are preventing the completion of assignments and/or session attendance or if a lack of motivation on the parent's part is relevant. Examples of the former might include illness of the parent or other family members, marital stress, or transportation difficulties. In any case, the therapist should emphasize the importance of attending the sessions and of completing the homework assignments. If motivational factors appear to be operating, then the therapist may wish to outline a set of contingencies for continued contact with the parent. This might include a monetary deposit to be refunded upon completion of the program, charging the parent for missed sessions, or terminating therapy if a predetermined number of assignments are not completed or sessions are missed. The use of a "parenting salary" is also an effective motivational strategy, especially with lower-class clients (Fleischman, 1979).

The Failure-to-Generalize Parent

A related but somewhat different issue is when parents have difficulty generalizing the parenting skills from the therapy situation to the real world. This occurs primarily in the first phase of the program where the parent learns to use attends and rewards effectively in a play situation (i.e., Child's Game) both in the clinic and at home, but not in daily interactions with the child.

The therapist's task with the parent who fails to generalize is to structure homework assignments such that the parent has to use the skills in everyday interactions with the child. This can best be done by increasing the number of positive child behavior programs (above the two or three that are typically requested) that the parent is required to develop and implement during the teaching of rewards. By helping the parent use the skills in multiple daily interactional situations, the therapist is essentially programming generalization.

The Personally Distressed Parent

Some parents who bring their children for treatment have problems themselves. These problems may involve depression, marital

distress, anxiety, or other disorders (see Chapter 6). Our assessment techniques are designed in part to detect such problems. If
parental personal adjustment problems do exist, our approach to
treatment depends on the severity of these difficulties. If our initial
assessment suggests that the problems are so severe as to most likely
interfere with parent training, we will refer the parent(s) for treatment of these problems. A decision as to whether to become involved in the parent training program can be made by the parent at
some later date. If the primary problems appear to be in the parent–child interaction and the parent's personal problems are not
severe, we will initiate the parent training program. Once we have
begun the program, we make every effort to complete it rather
than switching to treatment of some parent problem (e.g., depression) that may arise in the middle of the program. It has been our
experience on several occasions that as improvements in the parent–
child interaction have occurred, parental adjustment problems
have also improved. If a parent continues to experience personal
distress following completion of the parent training program, that
parent is referred for direct treatment of these difficulties.

Enuresis/Encopresis

During the course of the initial interview with the parent of a child
who has been referred for noncompliance and other behavior
problems, it is not uncommon to find that the child is also enuretic
or encopretic. Conversely, in the assessment of a child referred for
enuresis or encopresis, it may be concluded that problems in the
parent–child interaction, including child noncompliance, are occurring. In either situation, we typically postpone direct treatment
of the toileting problems until the parent is well into, or has completed, the parent training program.

This strategy is taken for several reasons. Most behavioral
toilet-training procedures require a modicum of child compliance
if they are to be successful (Doleys, 1979a, 1979b). For example,

the treatment program designed by Azrin, Sneed, and Foxx (1974) for enuresis requires that the parent have the child clean the soiled sheets, practice correct toileting procedures, and remake the bed. At the best of times, these procedures are likely to be unpleasant for both the parent and child. If the child is noncompliant, then these toileting procedures are likely to become the focus of a new source of conflict between parent and child; as a result, the toilet training is not likely to succeed. Even when the child is not particularly noncompliant, if the parent is unable to respond to appropriate toileting behavior with positive social reinforcement, then the program is, again, likely to fail.

In either situation, the parent training program provides the parent with the basic interactional skills needed to implement a toileting program. An additional incentive for first employing the parent training program is that, in some cases, it may remedy the enuresis and encopresis. In many of these cases, it seems that enuresis and encopresis are behavioral manifestations of extremely stressful parent–child conflicts. In other situations, the child's motivation for the inappropriate toileting behavior is more overt: to punish the parent by making it necessary to clean up the child's accidents. Regardless of the origin of the behavior, the parent training program is often a prerequisite for more formal treatment programs for enuresis and encopresis. Evaluation and treatment procedures for enuresis and encopresis have been presented by several investigators (Azrin & Foxx, 1974; Azrin, Hontos, & Besalel-Azrin, 1979; Doleys, 1979a, 1979b) and the interested reader is referred to their work.

The Role of Siblings

Many parent–child conflicts occur in the context of interactions between the referred child and a sibling. Especially when the referred child and the sibling are close in age, we often ask the parent to bring both children to the therapy sessions. There are a number of reasons for adopting this strategy. First, it may relieve any pressure that the referred child may be experiencing as *the* problem in the family, and it lends credence to the therapist's assertion that the focus of intervention will be on the parent–child(ren) interactions. Second, we have found that although only one of the children has been referred for treatment, a sibling often will display a very similar pattern of noncompliance and other deviant behavior (although perhaps at a lower intensity). Third, some of the referral problems may directly involve the sibling (e.g., fighting). Fourth, generalization may be programmed more effectively, since the parent will need to deal with both children's behaviors in the home setting. By learning to handle these situations in the clinic, the parent will be better equipped to deal with similar events at home. Finally, having the sibling present during treatment sessions may facilitate the effectiveness of some of the parenting techniques. For example, in the application of differential attention (i.e., reinforcement and ignoring), if one of the children is behaving inappropriately, then the parent ignores that child and reinforces the sibling for an incompatible appropriate behavior. This seems to facilitate the process in which the referred child (or sibling) learns the contingencies for various appropriate and inappropriate behaviors.

Initially, the parent should not practice the new skill in the therapy session with both children simultaneously. We have found that this situation is too complex and confusing for the parent. The parent should first practice the skill being taught individually with each child. Subsequently, practice can take place with both children together.

If it is not possible for both children to attend the sessions, all is not lost. As described in Chapter 6, we have found that even without training the parent to deal with an untreated sibling's problem behaviors, the parent is able to transfer these parenting skills to the sibling's behavior. Furthermore, the sibling responds by increasing his or her compliance to parental directions (Humphreys *et al.*, 1978).

Even in families in which a sibling's behavior is not problematic, it is important to emphasize to the parent that the skills being taught are ones that improve interactions between the parent and all children. Therefore, the parent should apply the procedures to all children who are in the appropriate age range. In some of our cases in which this has not been explicitly stated, parents have asked, "Is it all right to use the techniques with my other children?"

Situations Outside the Home

It is quite common for the parent to name at least one problematic situation with the referred child that occurs outside the home. The most frequently mentioned activities are riding in the car, going shopping or eating in restaurants, and visiting in others' homes. Although the circumstances vary tremendously depending upon the setting, there are several guidelines for handling problems that should be followed regardless of the particular setting. The first is that the parent should defer implementation of the parenting skills in these situations until a satisfactory level of success has been achieved employing the parenting procedures in the home. This is because the parent has less control of the environmental contingencies outside the home. If the parent is having problems employing the skills successfully at home, then it is almost guaranteed that any interventions in the car or at the grocery store will fail. In addition, by successfully employing parenting skills at home on a consistent basis, the parent increases the likelihood that these same procedures will be effective outside the home.

It is important that the parent realize that the same skills taught in the program for use at home can be employed to deal with difficulties outside the home. Attends and rewards should be used to reinforce appropriate child behaviors in these settings, while ignoring or a modified TO procedure can be employed to decrease inappropriate behaviors. Attending is especially helpful while riding in the car or shopping. If TO needs to be implemented, then the same command–warning–consequence sequence should be employed. However, the actual TO procedure may vary according to the setting. When in a store or restaurant, the parent may take the child out of the establishment and return to the car. The child can be placed in the car for 3 minutes and the parent can stand next to the car, or the child can be placed in the back seat and the parent can sit in the front seat. Once the TO period is completed, the parent and child return to the store, where the child is reinforced for appropriate behavior (walking in the aisle, eating quietly, etc.). When driving in the car, the parent can simply pull over to the side of the road and ignore the child until the inappropriate behavior subsides. At the homes of others, the same procedures for establishing a TO area in the child's own home would apply. The parent should anticipate whether TO may need to be used when visiting others and, if so, explain to the host that a TO procedure may be necessary for inappropriate behavior and may have to be implemented during the visit.

Finally, there are several other procedures that facilitate appropriate child behavior in settings outside the home. Prior to any excursion outside the home, the parent should explain to the child exactly what consequences will occur for inappropriate and appropriate behavior. This clearly delineates the rules to both the child and parent. It also is a good idea to have the parent employ brief "practice" sessions with the child in these settings. This is to assist the child in learning the desired behaviors and to increase the likelihood of a positive interaction between the parent and child. If riding in the car is a problem, then a quick ride through the neighborhood might be a first step, followed by subsequent rides of longer duration. Another tactic to facilitate longer car trips is for the parent to have a small set of toys (coloring books, cars and trucks, etc.) that are brought out only on these occasions. In this way, their novelty can be maintained for a longer time period. While shopping, involving the child in purchasing decisions is an excellent way to maintain good behavior and to begin consumer education at an early age. When visiting others, the parent should excuse himself or herself from the host to attend to the child on a frequent basis (see Chapter 3, "Rationale").

It should be noted that while the parenting procedures are generally the same as those that the parent has been taught to employ at home, the public context of these problematic situations can impede the consistent use of the procedures. The therapist should empathize with the parent concerning the difficulty of using the procedures outside the home; however, at the same time the importance of consistently employing the parenting procedures in these situations must be stressed. In this way, the overall positive aspects of the parent–child interaction will be markedly enhanced.

5

ADJUNCTIVE TREATMENTS

IN THIS CHAPTER, *we present two procedures we have developed to enhance generalization of our treatment effects. One procedure, developed primarily by Karen C. Wells, involves employing a self-control program with parents who participate in the parent training program. The second procedure, devised primarily by the second author (RJM), consists of giving the parent an extensive knowledge of social learning principles in addition to the parenting skills delineated in Chapters 3 and 4.*

Another variation of our parent training program has been to incorporate the parenting skills into a written brochure for parents interested in improving their children's mealtime behavior. This brochure was developed and evaluated as a model for how self-help programs can be used with common child behavior problems experienced by parents. The brochure, developed primarily by the second author, is presented in this chapter. The empirical evaluation of the three adjunctive treatments is discussed in Chapter 6.

USE OF A SELF-CONTROL PROGRAM WITH PARENTS

A review of the literature suggests that one strategy that may be particularly appropriate for enhancing changes in parenting be-

116

havior, and subsequently child behavior, is the use of self-control procedures. It has been proposed that changes in child behavior may not provide sufficient reinforcement to maintain good parenting behavior (Conway & Bucher, 1976). Similarly, after treatment particular individuals (e.g., spouses, next-door neighbors, grandparents) may undermine continued change efforts by failing to reinforce or by punishing treatment-acquired parenting skills (Marholin, Siegel, & Phillips, 1976). Self-control procedures may help circumvent these problems by teaching parents to provide themselves with antecedent and consequent events necessary to control their own behavior. In this way parents are no longer totally dependent on the external environment to continue to reinforce treatment-acquired skills. The program described in this chapter was developed and experimentally tested by Wells, Griest, and Forehand (1980). It is important to note that the self-control procedures are not part of our parenting program per se, but may be used as an adjunctive treatment to further facilitate child behavior change.

Our self-control training is designed to teach the parent self-monitoring and self-reinforcement skills. During the therapy sessions, the parent is given a multichannel wrist behavior counter capable of recording two categories of behavior. After being taught each parenting skill, the parent learns to accurately count the use of the skill. Initially, the parent is taught attending; subsequently, the parent is asked to self-monitor or count attends to the child on the wrist counter. The parent practices counting attends during a 10-minute role-play situation with the therapist in which the therapist plays the role of the child. Subsequently, the parent counts the number of attends used with the child during a 10-minute practice session in which the therapist observes the parent and child interacting and counts occurrences of attends. Such practice sessions continue until the parent obtains at least a 75% agreement with the therapist. Agreement is determined by using the following formulae:

$$\frac{\text{total \# of attends counted by the parent}}{\text{total \# of attends counted by the therapist}}$$

when the therapist's count is larger, and

$$\frac{1}{\dfrac{\text{total \# of attends counted by the parent}}{\text{total \# of attends counted by the therapist}}}$$

when the parent's count is larger. Subsequently, the parent is taught the rewarding skills and then is taught to self-monitor these skills in the same way that self-monitoring was taught for attending. As with attending, the practice sessions continue until the parent obtains at least 75% agreement with the therapist.

In Phase II of the parent training program, the parent learns the commanding and TO skills to criterion. Then the parent is taught to count the following parent–child interactive sequences: (1) alpha command (parent behavior), comply (child behavior), reward/attend (parent behavior), or alpha command (parent behavior), noncomply (child behavior), warning (parent behavior), comply (child behavior), reward/attend (parent behavior), on one behavior channel, and (2) alpha command (parent behavior), noncomply (child behavior), warning (parent behavior), noncomply (child behavior), TO (parent behavior) on the second behavior channel. The therapist initially prompts accurate self-monitoring in a role-play situation by informing the parent whenever one of these sequences occurs. Prompts are faded out as the parent begins to show proficiency in self-monitoring. Subsequently, the parent self-monitors during 10-minute practice periods with the child while the therapist observes the interaction and also counts occurrences of each of the two sequences. These practice sessions continue until the parent reaches a 75% accuracy criterion with the therapist.

In the last treatment session, the parent and therapist compose an individualized self-control program to be followed by the parent during the next 2-month period. First, a list of self-reinforcers is developed that includes material reinforcers (e.g., afternoon coffee break, special dessert) and high-probability behaviors (e.g., watching a favorite tv program, reading a favorite magazine) that can be applied daily, as well as three valued reinforcers (e.g., dinner out, shopping trip) that can be applied at 2- and 4-week intervals. Following this, the details of the program are outlined. Each day during the period that the program is in effect, the parent chooses a daily reinforcer from the list derived in the last session. Using a clock or timer for self-timing, the parent spends 15 minutes with the child in a potentially problematic situation (e.g., bath time, mealtime), reinforcing the child's appropriate behavior and providing consequences for child compliance and noncompliance. These behaviors are self-monitored using the wrist counter by recording each attending or rewarding response on one channel of the counter and interactive sequences in which TO occurs (i.e., command-noncomply-warning-noncomply-TO) on the second channel. Following each 15-minute "good parenting session," the parent self-administers the daily reinforcer only if (1) an average of at least four attends and/or rewards per minute was counted while the child was not in TO and (2) the parent reported that each occurrence of child noncompliance was handled appropriately (i.e., initially with a warning and then, if necessary, with TO). Although the parent is encouraged to employ treatment-acquired parenting skills as well as self-reinforcement throughout the day, these behaviors are self-monitored and recorded only during the daily 15-minute "good parenting sessions."

In order to motivate the occurrence of self-control behaviors (daily self-monitoring and self-reinforcement) and parenting sessions, each parent sets up a contract with the therapist after the details of the program have been explained. As part of the contract, the parent agrees to telephone in data from the daily 15-minute parenting sessions during the 2-month period according to the following schedule. The number of attends and rewards are reported as well as whether each act of child noncompliance was followed with TO.

First month—weeks 1 and 2. Parent telephones data into telephone answering service each night. An operator collects the self-monitored data as well as the occurrence or nonoccurrence of the daily self-reinforcement. First month — weeks 3 and 4. Parent telephones data in every other night. Second month — weeks 1 and 2. Parent telephones data in twice a week. Second month — weeks 3 and 4. Parent telephones data in on two occasions of own choosing.

The parent self-administers one of the three highly valued reinforcers after the first 2 weeks if the following criteria are met: called in data at least 75% of the required days and reached the criteria for daily self-reinforcement on at least 75% of these occasions. At the end of 4 weeks and 8 weeks the same criteria are imposed for receiving a preselected valued reinforcer.

The parent receives brief instructions by mail every 2 weeks, which (1) list daily reinforcers to be administered after parenting sessions, (2) inform the parent of the dates data are to be called in and (3) inform the parent that the criteria for 2-, 4-, and 8-week self-reinforcement have or have not been reached as agreed upon with the therapist in the last treatment session. An example of a letter sent at the beginning of the first 2-week period after the last treatment session is presented in Figure 5.1.

The self-control program is effective in facilitating child behavior change (see Chapter 6). The program obviously involves a number of procedures, including the parent learning to count the use of parenting skills, instructions to practice and count the skills at home, setting up rewards for use of the skills, and telephoning data to an answering service. Which of these components, individually or in combination, are the effective ingredient(s) is unknown. For clinical purposes, a therapist may choose to incorporate one or more of the components of the self-control program into the treatment package. For example, having the parent discriminate each occurrence of a particular parenting skill used and recording it may be beneficial, particularly for the parent who has difficulty identifying the occurrence of a behavior or a chain of behaviors that constitute a skill. However, it is important to reiterate that the effectiveness of the individual components of the self-control program is not known.

FIG. 5.1. SAMPLE LETTER SENT TO PARENT FOR FIRST 2-WEEK PERIOD

Mrs. Jane Doe
892 Smith Street
Athens, Georgia   30601

Dear Mrs. Doe:

Listed below is a summary of the contract that we made in our last treatment session. These instructions apply on a *daily* basis for the next 2 weeks.

1. *Every day* choose one "daily reward" for yourself from the following list. The one you choose should be something that you really want to do or have that day.

    a. crocheting   d. writing letters
    b. television   e. soaking in bathtub
    c. reading magazine or novel

2. Spend 15 minutes with Michael practicing the skills you learned (attending and rewarding compliance and appropriate behavior, using time-out for noncompliance). *Time yourself with a clock.* Remember to *wear your behavior counter* and count attends and rewards on one channel, and the number of times you use time-out with Michael on the second channel.

3. If you give at least four attends and rewards each minute that Michael is not in time-out (if he wasn't in time-out at all that would be a total of 60) *and* if you use time-out every time Michael disobeys you, then give yourself your daily reward. *Remember,* if you do not spend the 15 minutes practicing or do not meet the criteria just presented, you should *not* give yourself your daily reward.

4. Call the answering service every day after your parenting session. Tell the operator you are calling for Dr. Wells and state your name. Then give the operator the information asked for regarding parenting behavior.

Thank you for your continued cooperation.

Sincerely,

Karen C. Wells, Ph.D.

TEACHING PARENTS SOCIAL LEARNING PRINCIPLES

Another procedure that has been suggested as a potential means of enhancing generality is training parents in social learning principles in addition to behavioral parenting skills (Forehand & Atkeson, 1977; Nay, 1979). The reasons given for including formal training in social learning principles (O'Dell, Flynn, & Benlolo, 1977) have been that it is parsimonious in terms of time and effort (Patterson, Cobb, & Ray, 1973), parents need the theoretical framework supplied by such principles (Salzinger, Feldman, & Portnoy, 1970; Tharp & Wetzel, 1969), and generalization is more likely to occur (Forehand & Atkeson, 1977; Patterson et al., 1975; Weathers & Liberman, 1977). Patterson and his colleagues (Patterson et al., 1973, 1975) have been the strongest advocates of training parents in social learning principles prior to beginning treatment. They have stated that such training should allow the subsequent performance of child management skills to "a) accelerate more rapidly, b) display greater generalization in that parents are able to innovate a number of their own programs for both the target child and siblings, and c) be performed for a longer period following termination of the formal treatment program" (Patterson et al., 1975, p. 53).

In light of the potential benefits to be derived from this approach, we decided to develop a variation of our parent training program in which parents are not only taught the parenting skills but are given extensive background in the social learning principles on which the skills are based.[1] These principles include the hypoth-

---

1. It is important to note that the "basic" parent training program described in this book is based on, and utilizes, social learning principles. However, parental exposure to formal instruction in these principles is limited (see Chapter 4). The social learning principles training component that is outlined in this chapter represents both a more systematic and more extensive presentation of the principles than is employed in the basic parent training program.

esis that most social behavior is learned; characteristics, rules, types, and schedules of reinforcement; shaping; reciprocity; negative reinforcement; extinction; and punishment. The principles are described to the extent that they are consonant with the general framework of the parent training program. Thus, in many cases, the additional material elaborates on issues that are merely stated in the basic parent training program.

Instruction in social learning principles occurs via both didactic instruction by the therapist and brief reading assignments. The material for both types of instruction was selected from several behavioral parenting manuals. Specific reading assignments were drawn from the following sources: *Living with Children* (Patterson, 1976b), *Families: Applications of Social Learning to Family Life* (Patterson, 1975), *Parents Are Teachers: A Child Management Program* (Becker, 1971, 1975), and *Parent Manual on Child Rearing* (Wittes & Radin, 1968). Didactic instruction by the therapist is closely based on the material in the reading assignments, as well as drawn from other sources (Glogower & Sloop, 1976; Miller, 1975).

Instruction in specific social learning principles typically precedes training in the use of a particular technique. The reading assignments are distributed to the parent at the end of the session prior to the session in which the material is to be discussed. Relevant points from both sources are reiterated throughout the training as the skills are being applied. For example, the material concerning extinction is repeated and integrated into the teaching of the ignoring skill. To ensure that the parent is, in fact, learning these principles, he or she is required to meet specific criteria at three points in the treatment program: following the presentation of the rationale, following the presentation of the social learning principles appropriate for Phase I, and following the principles appropriate for Phase II. The criterion measurements are objective tests on which the parent is required to provide correct responses to at least 95% of the items. The parent is given three trials on which to do so.

Based on a content analysis of the incorrectly answered items, the therapist provides further instruction in the relevant principles and then readministers the incorrectly answered items. The number of trials to criterion is noted by the therapist. It has been our experience that three trials are sufficient for all parents to meet the criterion; most parents do so in one or two trials. The Social Learning Criterion Tests are based on the lecture material and reading assignments. Specific items were drawn from previously published tests of social learning material and the reading assignments (Becker, 1971, 1975; Clement, as noted in Glogower & Sloop, 1976; Patterson *et al.*, 1975) or were formulated by the second author (RJM). The Social Learning Criterion Tests and scoring keys are presented in Appendix D.

The reading assignments and didactic material for each of the major sections of the program ("Rationale," "Phase I: Differential Attention," "Phase II: Compliance Training") are described below. The points at which this didactic material and the Social Learning Criterion Tests are introduced into the basic parent training program are noted by referring to the outline of the program presented in Chapter 4. With respect to the reading assignments, the therapist should stress the importance of reading the assignments *before* coming to the next session, since these assignments form the basis of the upcoming didactic presentation. If the parent fails to complete the assignment, the therapist has the option of either postponing the session or having the parent read the assignment before the session begins.

Rationale

Reading Assignments

The initial reading assignments should be provided to the parent at the end of the final pretreatment home observation. (If home observations are not conducted, the assignments can be mailed or the parent can pick them up from the clinic a day or two prior to the first treatment session.) Both assignments provide an introduction to social learning. (Numbers in brackets refer to the order in which the assignments should be read.)

1. *Living with Children* (Patterson, 1976b, pp. 3-5, items 1-7 [1]).
2. *Families: Applications of Social Learning to Family Life* (Patterson, 1975, pp. 5-7 [2]).

Didactic Material

This should be presented in Session 1 as an elaboration of the rationale usually given for the program (presented in Chapter 4, p. 87, III. Rationale of program).

I. Social learning. (This is an elaboration of III.A. Behavior is learned and can be changed, p. 87.)
   A. Most behavior is learned (Wittes & Radin, 1968).
      1. People learn their behavior from other people.
      2. People teach, train, and change each other's behaviors.
      3. Parents and teachers teach, train, and change children.
      4. Adults teach, train, and change other adults (e.g., husbands teach wives and vice versa).
      5. Children teach, train, and change their parents!
   B. Social learning is concerned with how people teach people.
   C. It is important that you know how your behavior relates to and influences your child's behavior and how your child's behavior affects your behavior.
      1. People are often unaware of why they behave as they do.
      2. Both prosocial and problem behaviors are learned.
   D. Most people, *except parents,* are usually trained for the jobs at which they work. Parents are just expected to know how to raise their children successfully.
      1. We think parents should have the opportunity to learn to

use some of the methods that have been developed for teaching children.

2. Parents can learn how to establish behaviors in their children that will bring them success in school and in life. You do not have to trust to fate or to your instincts to develop successful behaviors in your children.

E. We will make use of social learning principles to help your child learn appropriate behaviors.

II. Potential negative effects of an overreliance on punishment. (This is an elaboration of III. D. 1. Discipline following noncompliance, p. 87.)

A. Extensive punishment sets up escape/avoidance behaviors that may be more harmful than the behavior being punished (Wittes & Radin, 1968).

B. Extensive punishment establishes emotional reactions, such as anxiety, for the child (Wittes & Radin, 1968).

C. Punishment may also make you feel guilty or upset if you punished because of anger or frustration.

D. Punishment will probably reduce noncompliance for a while, but we have found that the behavior is likely to reappear shortly after punishment occurs.

1. Punishment does not eliminate the child's motivation for engaging in a behavior (so when an opportunity next presents itself, the inappropriate behavior will reoccur).

2. For punishment to be effective, the behavior has to be punished every time. This is impossible (since you're not with the child every second), so the behavior actually gets stronger (we'll explain exactly how this occurs later in the program).

E. Punishment loses its effectiveness with frequent and continued use, so more and more severe punishments are required.

F. If physical punishment is overused, you may provide a model of aggression for the child.

G. You become less effective as a parent for the following
reasons.
   1. Your value as a positive influence on your child decreases,
   since you're always associated with punishment.
      a. Your child will avoid you.
      b. We also know that persons in the family who give out
      the most punishment receive the most punishment.
   2. Your control through punishment weakens as the punishment loses its effectiveness through too much use.

Social Learning Criterion

The Social Learning Criterion, Rationale Test (see Appendix D)
should be administered after the rationale of the program (Session
1, III. Rationale of program, p. 87) has been presented. The
parent should be told that the purpose of the test is to make sure
that the principles are understood before the program continues.
The therapist should state that it is not a test per se, but rather a
way for him or her to determine which areas should receive the
most attention.

Phase I

Reading Assignments

These materials should be distributed to the parent at the end
of V. Mechanics of the program, p. 87, in Session 1. The reading materials discuss characteristics, rules, types, and schedules
of positive reinforcement, reciprocity, and the "criticism trap."

   1. *Parents Are Teachers: A Child Management Program*
   (Becker, 1971, pp. 35-41 [3]; pp. 85-88 [7]; Unit 6 Review
   Sheet [8]). Assignment 8 is from Becker's (1975) *Review Tests
   for Parents Are Teachers.*
   2. *Living with Children* (Patterson, 1976b, pp. 25-26, items

1-6, p. 29 [5]; pp. 31-37, items 1, 3-6, 11-31 [6]).
3. *Parent Manual on Child Rearing* (Wittes & Radin, 1968, pp. 7-10 [4].

Didactic Material

This should be presented at the beginning of Phase I (Session 1, VI. Phase I, p. 88).

I. All behavior is maintained, changed, or shaped by the effects (consequences) of the behavior.
   A. These consequences either strengthen (reward or reinforce) or weaken the behavior.
   B. To strengthen a behavior, reinforce or reward it.
   C. A behavior can be weakened by no longer reinforcing it.
II. Based on the positive reinforcement rule and the attention rule (VI. A.2. Explain two assumptions on which Phase I is based), the following are critical to improving your child's behavior.
   A. Focus on strengthening a desirable behavior that is likely to be rewarding to your child and that, at the same time, will compete with the undesirable behavior that you are weakening and eventually take its place (the child can't do both behaviors at the same time).
   B. If you pay attention to your child when the child is being good (i.e., compliant), then it is more likely that the child will engage in that behavior more frequently.
   C. At the same time, if you don't give the child attention (i.e., if the child is ignored) when he or she is engaging in bad behavior, then these bad behaviors are not as likely to occur in the future and will eventually stop.
      1. Extinction (ignoring) is the one method that eventually eliminates a behavior completely, since the child learns that there is absolutely no payoff for engaging in the behavior.

2. For ignoring to be effective, the parent must ignore the behavior every time it occurs.

3. *Therapist note:* When the parent first starts to ignore, there may be an initial burst of inappropriate behavior.

   a. This is normal as the child is testing limits.

   b. The parent must be consistent.

D. The opposite is also true.

1. If you ignore (i.e., don't reinforce) your child when he or she is being good, you will get less good behavior.

   a. Some old adages do *not* apply.

     (1) The child is "supposed to know" which behaviors are appropriate; therefore, she or he is expected to engage in those behaviors. But the only way the child knows whether to engage in a behavior is if that behavior has been reinforced in the past.

     (2) "Leave well enough alone" and "Let sleeping dogs lie" will only result in the good behavior eventually disappearing.

   b. A new adage does apply: "Catch your child being good" (Becker, 1971). Too often we tend to take good behavior for granted.

2. Paying attention to your child (watching, discussing, smiling, yelling, nagging, criticizing, etc.) when she or he is displaying inappropriate behavior will make that behavior more likely to occur in the future.

   a. We all frequently reward undesirable behavior accidentally/unintentionally by occasionally "giving in" (paying attention to it), even though we "know better." This occasional reinforcement will cause the behavior to persist.

   b. Children do the same thing to us (they don't intend to reinforce us for scolding, but this happens when we scold since they stop the inappropriate behavior briefly).

       c. This situation is called the "criticism trap" (Becker, 1971, 1975), since the parent thinks criticism (negative attention such as scolding, nagging, etc.) is effective because the child stops the inappropriate behavior for a while. Thus, the parent uses criticism whenever possible. However, by paying attention to inappropriate behavior, this makes it more likely that the child will misbehave again.

       d. The end result is that home is not a very pleasant place, since the parent must always be ready with scolding, nagging, or criticizing.

  E. *Therapist note:* Use both positive and negative examples from the parent's and child's in-session behavior or from parent report data to illustrate the role of parental attention in influencing the child's behavior.

  F. Once you realize how you are reinforcing your child, you can start to weaken undesirable behavior and strengthen socially desirable behavior.

III. The following are characteristics of positive reinforcement. (This represents an elaboration of Session 4, II. Rewards, presented on p. 90.) The ultimate goal of parental reinforcement is for the appropriate child behaviors that are reinforced to eventually become self-reinforcing to the child. In this way, the child will develop control over his or her own behavior.

  A. Reinforcement should follow *immediately* after good behavior. If delayed, then it is possible that some other child behavior (which may be good or bad) actually will be reinforced.

  B. Be *specific*—tell your child exactly what behavior you're reinforcing (you will use attends and labeled rewards to do this).

  C. Reinforcement can be continuous (continuous reinforcement) or only occasional (intermittent reinforcement).

    1. Continuous reinforcement is given every time the behavior occurs.

    a. It is an excellent procedure for starting or strenghening a behavior.

    b. Changes in behavior are more likely to occur if reinforcement is *consistent*. The behavior must be reinforced more than one time.

2. Intermittent reinforcement follows continuous reinforcement success.

    a. It is given occasionally after the behavior occurs and in an unpredictable manner.

    b. It is excellent for maintaining a behavior once the behavior is well established since it is very resistant to extinction.

    c. Intermittent reinforcement applies to negative behaviors as well. If you *occasionally* pay attention to inappropriate behavior, then the negative behavior is strengthened and is stronger than if you reinforced it every time.

3. A short summary of positive reinforcement follows.

    a. In the early stages of learning a task, reinforce every correct response.

    b. As the behavior becomes stronger, require more and more correct responses before reinforcing (gradually shift to unpredictable intermittent reinforcement).

    c. "To get it going, reward every time. To keep it going, reward intermittently" (Becker, 1971, p. 38).

D. Social reinforcers are in contrast to material reinforcers.

1. There are two general types of rewards, social and material (nonsocial).

    a. Social reinforcers involve the parent's behavior (saying or doing something to the child).

    b. Material reinforcers involve such things as money, tokens, privileges, candy, and the like.

2. Social reinforcers are more versatile than material reinforcers.

    a. Social reinforcers are always available as immediate

consequences of good behavior, while this is not necessarily the case with material reinforcers.

b. Social reinforcers are useful for starting *and* critical for maintaining good behavior, while material reinforcers are not as effective in maintaining good behavior.

c. We have an endless supply of social reinforcers, but this is not the case with material reinforcers (e.g., money).

d. Social reinforcers are what the child can expect to find in the real world as reinforcement for social behavior.

3. Since social reinforcers are more useful and versatile, we will be working with them.

E. Appropriate reinforcers must be employed.

1. It is very important that the reinforcer the parent uses is, in fact, reinforcing to the child.

2. The reinforcer should also be of appropriate magnitude for the particular behavior.

a. If the reinforcer is too large, the child will become tired of it quickly (satiation), and it will no longer serve as a reinforcer.

b. If the reinforcer is too small, it will not motivate the child to change the behavior.

F. Shaping (successive approximations) is useful when dealing with complex behaviors.

1. When the child is learning a new behavior (particularly a complicated one), he or she should be reinforced for each small step along the way that approximates the goal rather than as a prize at the very end.

2. If the task is too big, the child may have to wait too long for reinforcement.

3. Shaping sets the child up for success, since the child is being reinforced for trying and for improvements toward the goal.

4. Shaping can also establish work habits and responsibilities for later, since the child will learn to keep trying until he or she has mastered a task.
5. Shaping requires patience, since it is often easier in the short run for the parent to do a task for the child. However, in the long run, this may make the child dependent.

G. Reciprocity refers to the idea that, in terms of interactions among family members, "You get what you give" (Patterson, 1975, p. 20).

1. It is not just children who are taught by reinforcement. Children influence parents' behavior as well.
   a. The criticism trap is one example.
   b. Children also influence adult behavior by positive reinforcement.
2. Everyone (adults as well as children) has to receive at least a minimal amount of social reinforcement. If you don't, you will probably become depressed.
   a. Many parents are in this situation since they may get little or no social reinforcement from their child or spouse (they may be divorced, spouse may be too busy with job, etc.).
   b. If a parent is not getting much social reinforcement, that parent is not likely to *give* it to a child or spouse.
3. The following points are made in summary of the idea of reciprocity.
   a. The person in the family who gives the most reinforcement/punishment receives the most reinforcement/punishment.
   b. To receive a positive input from another family member, you have to give one first.
   c. If you give a negative input to another family member, then you should expect one in return. Unfortunately, this is much more likely to be reciprocated than a positive input (Miller, 1975).

Social Learning Criterion

The instrument should be administered at the conclusion of the preceding didactic material. The Social Learning Criterion, Phase I Test and scoring key are in Appendix D.

Phase II

Reading Assignments

The materials are distributed at the end of the last complete session of Phase I. The reading assignments discuss the potential negative effects of punishment, how to use effective punishment, and indications for its use.

1. *Parent Manual on Child Rearing* (Wittes & Radin, 1968, pp. 15–18 [9]).
2. *Parents Are Teachers: A Child Management Program* (Becker, 1971, pp. 121–128 [10]).

Didactic Material

This is presented in Phase II after the command training segment (Session 7, IV. C. Introduce consequences for noncompliance, p. 95).

I. Commands and Shaping
   A. If the behavior you desire is relatively complex, break it down into the smaller units or steps necessary to achieve that behavior. Remember, we talked about shaping (successive approximations) by reinforcement? The same applies here.
   B. Examples at home include the following.
      1. Rather than to say "Pick up all the toys," say, "Put the three blocks in the box," or "Put the cars in the box," and the like.

2. Rather than to say "Make your bed," say, "Pull the sheet up first," "Now pull the blanket up," and so forth.

II. Effective Punishment

A. Punishment is an event that occurs following a behavior; it weakens the future rate of the behavior (Becker, 1971, p. 121). It involves the presentation of negative consequences or the withdrawal of reinforcers.

B. As noted earlier, punishment is not the preferred mode of interacting with the child. Briefly review the potential negative effects of punishment (see pp. 126–127).

C. Use of punishment per se is not immoral. There are times that punishment *is* necessary and is the most appropriate action to take.

   1. Punishment is appropriate in an emergency to save the child from danger (e.g., in careless crossing of the street) (Wittes & Radin, 1968).

   2. When the inappropriate behavior is so frequent that there is not any good behavior to reinforce, punishment may be necessary.

   3. When reinforcement will not be effective because it is less pleasurable for the child than the inappropriate behavior in which he or she is engaging, punishment may be needed (Wittes & Radin, 1968).

D. Generally, however, punishment should be used as little as possible.

E. Most of the rules regarding effective punishment are similar to those for reinforcement. Effective punishment (Becker, 1971, p. 127) is characterized by the following conditions.

   1. Is given immediately.

   2. Relies on taking away reinforcers and provides a clear-cut method for earning them back.

   3. Includes a verbal warning signal. This eventually serves as a cue and helps develop internal controls so that external controls like punishment are needed much less often.

4. Is carried out in a calm, matter-of-fact way.

5. Is given along with much reinforcement for behaviors incompatible with the punished behavior.

6. Is consistent. The procedure is carried out the same way each time, and reinforcement is not given for the punished behavior. Remember, if you aren't consistent, you may end up making the behavior worse.

III. The punishment procedure we recommend and which you will learn here is called time-out (TO), which is short for time-out from positive reinforcement.

Social Learning Criterion

The instrument should be administered at the conclusion of the preceding didactic material. The Social Learning Criterion, Phase II Test and scoring key are presented in Appendix D.

A SELF-ADMINISTERED PROGRAM TO IMPROVE CHILDREN'S MEALTIME BEHAVIOR

In recent years there has been an abundance of self-help behavior therapies that can be totally self-administered and require little, if any, professional consultation (Rosen, 1976, 1977). These programs are usually in the form of written materials of some type (books, brochures, etc.). Their primary advantage is that they enable therapists to extend their services to a greater number of individuals with minimal increments in professional time. We have stressed the importance of empirically validating these self-help programs for parents (McMahon & Forehand, 1980, 1981).

Within the area of parent training, self-administered behavior therapies are now coming into vogue (see McMahon & Forehand, 1980, for a review). Several books and manuals for parents have appeared in the last decade concerning various approaches to child rearing (e.g., Becker, 1971; Patterson, 1975). However, as Risley *et al.* (1976) have noted, these books have tended to advocate general approaches to child rearing. It seems to be potentially more beneficial to address advice systems to more specific problems and settings within the home (Risley *et al.*, 1976). Also, by delivering parent training materials directly to the home, the issue of setting generality from the clinic to the home (see Chapter 6) is eliminated.

One area in which a self-administered therapeutic intervention seems appropriate is children's mealtime behaviors. The importance of mealtime as an opportunity for the child to learn social, interactional, and cultural values has long been stressed (Dreyer & Dreyer, 1973). Surprisingly, there has been little research in modifying inappropriate mealtime behaviors in the normal child, although experts in child development have stated that the preschool child often engages in messy table behavior, leaving the table, and excessive demands for attention during meals (Ames, 1970; Breckenridge & Vincent, 1965).

The purpose of this section is to present a brochure we have developed and evaluated to teach parents to improve their preschool children's inappropriate mealtime behaviors. A slight variation of this program on mealtime behavior has been demonstrated by McMahon and Forehand (1978) to be effective with nonclinic-referred children when used alone (i.e., with no therapist–client contact) (see Chapter 6). The program can be used as a supplement to the parent training program or can be used independently of the program in situations where the assessment procedures (see Chapter 2) indicate no problems in parent–child interaction except in a circumscribed situation (i.e., mealtime).

The program for mealtime behavior described in this chapter can be viewed as an example of how written materials can be developed and evaluated for other specific child behavior problems in the home (e.g., bedtime, bath time, guests visiting in the home). Although the procedures used with other problem behaviors would be similar to those used with mealtime problems, empirical data to support the effectiveness of such programs have not yet been collected.

The first step in the mealtime program is to have the parent complete the Mealtime Behavior Checklist (Figure 5.2). This checklist includes a number of behaviors that have been identified in the literature as inappropriate mealtime behaviors (e.g., Barton, Guess, Garcia, & Baer, 1970; O'Brien & Azrin, 1972). These behaviors are grouped into "Inappropriate Eating Behaviors" and "Misconduct." In addition, the parent may add other inappropriate behaviors not covered on the list. The brochure is then given to the parent, who is asked to implement the procedures in the home at mealtime. The Mealtime Behavior Checklist serves as a prompt for the parent to implement the program procedures for the noted inappropriate mealtime behaviors. The TO procedure described in the brochure is somewhat different from the one taught in the parenting program. Since the brochure is often used in a totally self-administered context, the TO procedure has been simplified so that there are fewer steps involved.

The Brochure: "How to Handle Your Child's
Inappropriate Mealtime Behaviors"
by Robert J. McMahon, Ph.D., and
Rex L. Forehand, Ph.D.

In order to correct your child's inappropriate mealtime behaviors, it is very important that you decide which specific behaviors you wish to change. The list of your child's mealtime behaviors that you decided were inappropriate is included at the end of this brochure.

As a parent, your attention to your child is very important to him or her. Children quickly learn that they receive attention for some things they do. These behaviors are the ones that your child will do again and again. Therefore, it is important that you give attention to your child only when the child is behaving correctly at

FIG. 5.2. MEALTIME BEHAVIOR CHECKLIST

I. Inappropriate Eating Behaviors

_____ 1. Spilling food onto the table and/or floor on purpose

_____ 2. Eating food spilled on the table, floor, or clothing

_____ 3. Eating food by placing mouth directly on it (without use of fingers or utensils)

_____ 4. Eating too fast (not pausing between bites)

_____ 5. Putting too much food in mouth, such that chewing cannot be done with the mouth closed

_____ 6. Playing with food (e.g., patting Jello with hands, smearing food)

_____ 7. Eating food with fingers (excepting use of fingers to hold foods properly eaten with fingers; e.g., sandwiches, potato chips, etc.)

_____ 8. Removing food from the mouth (spitting out or using fingers)

_____ 9. Using fingers to place food on utensil

_____ 10. Others:

II. Misconduct

_____ 1. Not coming to the table when called

_____ 2. Standing up or leaving table before end of meal

_____ 3. Stealing food or other objects at the table

_____ 4. Throwing or banging utensils

_____ 5. Throwing food

_____ 6. Pushing the table

_____ 7. Rocking or moving the chair (other than to sit down or leave the table)

_____ 8. Placing a foot on the table

_____ 9. Placing head on the table

_____ 10. Placing a foot on others or their chairs, or kicking them

_____ 11. Hitting others at the table

_____ 12. Whining or crying

_____ 13. Screaming or yelling

_____ 14. Others:

the table. There are two primary ways in which you should respond positively.

1. Praise your child acting appropriately at the table (e.g., "You're such a good boy [or girl] for eating your food!"). See the attached list for some more praise statements.
2. Give physical rewards such as a hug, kiss, pat, and so forth.

These two types of positive attention from you, especially the praise, are very important in helping good behavior get started and in maintaining this good behavior once it has begun.

Initially, it is important to praise your child quite often when he or she is acting appropriately at the table. Therefore, for the first week during a meal you should praise your child at least once every minute (more frequently if you wish) that he or she has acted appropriately. During the next week, you might praise the child a little less often. Never phase out your praise statements completely — always praise your child several times during every meal when he or she is being good.

We feel that the best way to establish a good relationship with your child and to eliminate the child's bad behavior at the table is by rewarding him or her for being good. However, there are times when you may need a punishment procedure to stop this bad behavior. In order to implement the following procedure, it is necessary that you use a quiet room, such as a bathroom or bedroom, where you can place your child when he or she misbehaves at the table. The room should contain as few fun things (such as magazines, toys, tv) as possible. Furthermore, there should not be dangerous items like sharp objects and medicine in the room.

Use the following procedure when your child misbehaves at the table. (Note: Please use this procedure only when your child does one of the specific behaviors you listed earlier as a behavior problem; see the attached list.)

1. Tell him or her to stop misbehaving. Be sure to name the bad behavior. Tell your child only once, and make your state-

ment as brief as possible. For example, say, "[Child's name], stop throwing food right now!" If he or she complies (e.g., stops throwing food), reward your child. For example, say, "That's a good boy [or girl] for doing what Mom asks you to do."

2. If your child does not comply immediately or complies for a moment and then does the same behavior again (say within 5 seconds), immediately take the child firmly by the hand and lead him or her to the quiet room, and while placing him or her in the quiet room say, "You didn't do what I said, so you have to stay in here." Be sure not to say anything else to your child at any time during this procedure. You don't owe your child any additional explanations.

3. Then close the door and hold it if necessary to keep the child in the room. Leave the child in the quiet room for 3 minutes, but be sure to wait until he or she has quiet crying, fussing, or yelling for 15 seconds at the end of the 3-minute period before taking him or her out. It is important that you do not respond in any way (such as talking to the child) while the child is in the room.

4. When taking the child out, open the door and say, "Now we will finish eating."

5. As soon as your child is acting appropriately at the table, *praise* him or her for the good table behavior.

6. If your child begins to act inappropriately at the table again, follow the above procedure, even if you have just brought him or her back to the table.

At first, you will find this procedure difficult to implement. However, once your child realizes that you are going to be consistent and not tolerate bad behavior at the table *(and that you will reward good behavior)*, life will be much easier at mealtime and you will enjoy your child more.

Some Praise Statements

1. "I really like it when you eat so nicely."
2. "You are such a big boy [or girl] to eat your food."
3. "Thank you for behaving so well at the table."
4. "I'm so proud of you—you're acting just like a grown-up."

5. "I like it when you stay at the table for Mom."
6. "You have such good manners—that's great."
7. "Thank you." "You're so nice!" "Good!"

These are just a few examples of some praise statements you can make to reward your child for good mealtime behavior. Don't be afraid to use other statements of your own.

6

REVIEW OF
THE TREATMENT
RESEARCH

T HE PRECEDING CHAPTERS *present how to assess and treat child noncompliance and related problem behaviors. In this chapter, we describe the research that we have conducted in order to provide an empirical basis for our procedures. We view this chapter as "must reading," since the therapist implementing the program needs to know the data on which the treatment procedures are based.*

Research pertaining to the effectiveness of the treatment program has been undertaken in four stages. First, various components of the program have been examined individually in a series of laboratory investigations in order to specify the variables in the parent training package that are effective in modifying child noncompliance. Second, the immediate outcome of using the program with noncompliant children was examined in several investigations. Third, the generality of treatment effects across settings, time, siblings, and behavior has been determined. Included as part of the generality studies are data addressing whether the generalized changes are socially valid. Finally, procedures for enhancing generality have been examined. This chapter presents a review of the research conducted in these four areas.

LABORATORY INVESTIGATIONS

As just mentioned, in order to specify the parameters and variables in the parent training package that are effective in modifying noncompliance, various components of the program have been investigated in a laboratory setting. Use of such a setting has allowed the control of extraneous variables that may systematically or unsystematically affect child compliance in the home. Furthermore, more closely supervised introduction as well as withdrawal of treatment conditions (e.g., ABAB designs) has been possible. These studies were conducted with children who were not referred to clinics for treatment. The selection of nonclinic children for these studies was a function of experimenter convenience, as subjects could be recruited and paid for their participation. In addition, ethical questions concerning research with subjects who are seeking treatment were eliminated.

All of the studies described in this section were conducted in laboratory settings equipped with observation windows and adjoining observation rooms. Children who participated in these investigations were 4 to 6 years old. In all cases, the experimenter used a bug-in-the-ear to cue the parent how to respond to the child.

In one study, Bernhardt and Forehand (1975) examined the effects of different types of parental social reinforcement upon the child's response. A game that involved dropping marbles in a hole was used. Forty mothers and their children were assigned to one of two groups. Following a baseline in which the mother simply observed her child drop marbles in either of two holes (designated as the red and green holes) for 3 minutes, the mother was cued by an experimenter to reward the child on an FR 2 schedule (i.e., every second response was reinforced) during a 6-minute period for dropping a marble in the hole least preferred during baseline. For one group, each mother used unlabeled verbal rewards (e.g., "Very good"), whereas in the second group mothers used labeled verbal rewards (e.g., "Very good, you put another marble in the red hole"). Relative to baseline, both reward conditions were associated with increases in the number of marbles dropped in the rewarded hole; however, the labeled reinforcement was associated with a significantly greater increase from baseline to treatment than the unlabeled condition. These results suggest the importance of labeling verbal reinforcement given to children and support the efficacy of teaching parents the use of labeled verbal rewards in the first phase of the treatment program.

In an effort to investigate the effects of number of parental commands upon child compliance as well as investigating certain parameters of the compliant act itself, Forehand and Scarboro (1975) had mothers issue 12 standard commands to their children in a laboratory setting. Presence or absence of compliance was coded for each of 15 intervals of 10 seconds following each command. A comparison of child compliance to the first six versus the second six commands indicated significantly less compliance to the latter commands. Furthermore, children demonstrated significantly less compliance in each of the first 3 intervals of 10 seconds following a command than in the latter (4–15) intervals. The first result suggests that as the number of parental commands increases, the amount of child compliance decreases. Such a finding lends support for the first component of the parent training program in which parents are initially taught to reduce the number of commands to their children. The second finding suggests that failure to initiate compliance rather than failure to continue or complete the compliant act is a major factor in the occurrence of noncompliance. Thus, as is done in the treatment program, attempts to increase compliance should focus on the initiation of compliance.

The majority of our laboratory studies have examined the effects of TO on child noncompliance to maternal commands (Gardner, Forehand, & Roberts, 1976; Scarboro & Forehand, 1975). The studies were undertaken after a review of the literature indicated that most investigators utilizing TO have not employed adequate experimental methodology (Forehand & MacDonough, 1975) and that most parameters of TO (e.g., location of TO, presence versus absence of a verbalized reason for TO prior to its onset) have not been examined (MacDonough & Forehand, 1973). As TO is one of the primary skills taught in Phase II of the parent training program, it was decided that a systematic examination of the procedure and its various parameters was needed.

Scarboro and Forehand (1975) compared within-room (ignoring) and out-of-room (isolation) TO procedures. After a baseline, mothers assigned to the within-room procedure were instructed to issue a warning ("If you do not _____, I am not going to play with you for a while") if the child did not initiate compliance within 5 seconds after a maternal command. If the child did not initiate compliance within 5 seconds after the warning, the mother moved away from the child and withdrew all her attention from him or her for 2 minutes. After 2 minutes, the mother returned her attention to the child when the child was quiet for 5 seconds (5-second quiet contingency). The procedure for the out-of-room TO was similar except for the warning ("If you do not _____, I am going to take the toys and leave the room") and the actual TO administration, which involved the mother taking the toys and leaving the room for 2 minutes plus the 5-second quiet contingency. During training, mothers in both groups were cued by way of the bug-in-the-ear as to when and how to issue commands and warnings and to implement TO. Relative to a control group in which the mothers issued the same commands but did not use TO, both TO procedures significantly increased initiation of compliance to maternal commands. The two procedures did not differentially affect compliance. However, the within-room procedure required significantly more administrations of TO than the out-of-room procedure, suggesting that the latter is more efficient than the former.

Efficiency is particularly important when one considers that potential sources of reinforcement are being lost with multiple administrations of TO. Finally, in a posttraining period, without cueing from the experimenter regarding when to issue warnings or implement TO, the mothers in both TO groups maintained child compliance at the levels previously achieved during training.

The efficacy of including a verbalized reason (e.g., "You did not do what I said, so I am going to take all the toys and not play with you") in the TO procedure was examined by Gardner *et al.* (1976). A comparison of groups receiving TO only, verbalized reason followed by TO, and TO followed by a verbalized reason failed to reveal any significant differences; however, all three were associated with less noncompliance than a control group for which TO was not implemented. During a posttraining period without cueing from the experimenter about when to implement TO, the mothers in the TO groups maintained their children's compliance at the level obtained during training.

Hobbs, Forehand, and Murray (1978) have produced results that suggest that the length of TO is a critical variable in the effectiveness of TO in suppressing noncompliance. In this study, children were assigned to a control group or one of three experimental groups, consisting of 10 seconds, 1 minute, or 4 minutes of TO (standing in a corner) for each noncompliance to a series of maternal commands. The 4-minute TO was more effective in reducing noncompliance than the 10-second or 1-minute TO and all were more effective than a control group in which TO was not implemented. During a subsequent treatment withdrawal period (return to baseline), the noncompliance of the subjects in the 4-minute TO group was significantly lower than that of the 10-second or 1-minute TO groups. The results indicate that a TO period as brief as 1 minute is not as effective as a TO of moderate duration (i.e., 4 minutes) in suppressing and maintaining noncompliance.

An earlier study by Hobbs and Forehand (1975) suggested that contingent release from TO is also important when modifying noncompliance. A comparison of contingent release (15 seconds of quiet were required prior to the mother re-entering the room in an out-of-room TO procedure) and noncontingent release (subjects were yoked to those in the contingent release group in terms of the total length of TO, but no quiet contingency was employed) groups indicated that less disruption occurred during TO for the contingent release group. Furthermore, the results suggested that contingent release was associated with less noncompliance to maternal commands than noncontingent release.

These TO studies suggest that the most effective and efficient TO condition is one in which the parent removes the child from all sources of reinforcement rather than just ignoring the child, uses a TO duration longer than 1 minute (but for ethical reasons under 5 minutes), and releases the child from TO when the child is being quiet. A verbalized reason for TO is optional, as it neither adds to nor subtracts from the effectiveness of TO in suppressing child noncompliance. We teach the parent to use a verbalized reason, since most parents feel more comfortable in utilizing the TO procedure with their child when this is done.

One recent study has examined the interactive effects of two of the parenting skills in the parent training program on noncompliance. Roberts *et al.* (1978) trained one group of mothers to issue alpha commands and one group in command giving plus TO training. The results indicated that both types of training increased child compliance relative to a placebo–control condition. However, the combination of command training and TO training was more effective than command training alone, suggesting the importance of consequences and antecedents in modifying child noncompliance.

IMMEDIATE OUTCOME STUDIES

The laboratory investigations present data clearly indicating the importance of parental use of alpha commands, social reinforcement, and TO in modifying child noncompliance. In addition to the examination of the various components of the treatment program in the laboratory setting, several early studies were conducted in which the effectiveness of the entire parent training program was evaluated. Each of these studies limited behavioral assessment of treatment outcome to the clinic laboratory setting.

In one early outcome study, Forehand and King (1974) successfully used the parent training program to treat eight preschool noncompliant children and their mothers in a mean of 6.2 sessions. In the Child's Game (free-play situation), mothers significantly increased their use of rewards and significantly decreased their use of commands and questions from baseline to treatment. In the Parent's Game (parental control situation), maternal rewards again increased significantly from baseline to treatment, as did child compliance. These results suggest that both parent and child behaviors changed in the desired and predicted direction with treatment.

Forehand and King (1977) subsequently used the program in the treatment of 11 preschool children and their mothers. Parent perception measures (the scales of the Parent Attitudes Test) as well as observational data on the mother–child interaction in the clinic were obtained. Results of the parent perception measures indicated that after treatment the mothers perceived their children as significantly better adjusted than prior to treatment. The results of the observational measures were similar to those obtained by Forehand and King (1974): mothers significantly decreased their use of commands and questions and significantly increased their use of rewards, and children increased their compliance to commands. Improvements in maternal perception of the child and the maternal and child behaviors were maintained at a 3-month follow-up. Relative to a nonclinic "normal" sample of 11 mother–child pairs, the treated children were less compliant prior to treatment and more compliant after treatment. Furthermore, prior to treatment mothers of the clinic children perceived their children as less well-adjusted than mothers of the nonclinic children perceived their children. However, following treatment, the two groups of parents did not differ significantly in their perceptions of their children.

The program's effectiveness is not limited to modifying the interactional patterns of physically normal children and their parents. Although they defined their behavioral categories in a slightly different manner, Hanf and Kling (1973), at the University of Oregon Medical School, have used the same procedures to alter the interactions between 40 pairs of mothers and their severely physically handicapped, noncompliant children. A comparison of baseline to treatment data indicated that the mothers significantly increased their use of verbal rewards and decreased their use of commands and questions. There also was a significant increase in child compliance. All gains were maintained at a 3-month follow-up. In a case study, Forehand, Cheney, and Yoder (1974) reported similar effects in the treatment of a noncompliant deaf child.

OUTCOME STUDIES EXAMINING GENERALIZATION

Although the earlier outcome studies suggested the immediate effectiveness of the treatment program in improving parent–child interactions in a clinic setting, lack of proper experimental control and failure to assess parent and child behavior outside the clinic setting limited the conclusions regarding the efficacy of the program. Of primary importance, then, was the need to assess the generalization of these treatment effects across settings (from clinic to home and school), time (after termination of treatment), behaviors (from treated to untreated behaviors), and siblings (from treated to untreated children), and to determine whether these effects were socially valid. Generality is important for the success of a parent training program from at least two perspectives (Forehand & Atkeson, 1977). From a treatment viewpoint, generality results in a more optimal use of therapist time, since the therapist will no longer be required to treat recurrences of previously treated problems, problem behaviors in new settings, all of the problem behaviors of the child, or the behavior problems of the child's siblings. From a prevention viewpoint, generalization minimizes repeated professional intervention and should result in a diminution of future behavior problems of the child (and sibling). This would allow clinicians to move from a focus on tertiary prevention (i.e., the treatment of problem behaviors) to one of primary prevention (e.g., the enhancement of living conditions) (Caplan, 1964). An additional reason for assessing generality is that it allows therapists to monitor the potential occurrence of any "negative, second-order, or unintended" (Graziano, 1977, p. 281) side effects of parent training.

Generalization to the Home Setting

In order to evaluate the effectiveness of the treatment program in comparison to a no-treatment control group and to investigate the generality of treatment changes from the clinic to the home, Peed et al. (1977) undertook a study that compared six mother–child pairs who received treatment by way of the parent training program to six mother–child pairs who constituted a waiting list control group. Each mother–child pair was randomly assigned to either the treatment or control group after the mother contacted our clinic expressing concern about her child's noncompliance. Each mother–child pair then underwent pretreatment sets of clinic and home observations. Following treatment or a waiting period of similar length, each mother–child pair again underwent the clinic and home observations (hereafter referred to as "posttreatment"). By assessing maternal and child behavior in both the clinic and home settings, the setting generality of the parenting program could be examined.

The results from the Peed et al. (1977) study indicated that in the Child's Game in the clinic setting, the mothers in the treatment group significantly decreased their frequency of questions and significantly increased their frequency of attends and rewards from pre- to posttreatment assessments. In the Parent's Game in the clinic setting, the treatment group mothers decreased their use of beta commands and increased their use of contingent attention for child compliance from pre- to posttreatment. The children demonstrated a significant increase in compliance in the Parent's Game. Thus, these data replicated earlier findings of improved mother and child behavior in the clinic setting. Of primary importance were the data concerning generalization of these treatment effects to the home setting. In the home observations, significant increases from the pre- to posttreatment assessments occurred for child compliance and for maternal rewards, attends, and contingent attention to compliance. Significant decreases occurred for maternal use of beta commands. For the control group significant changes did not occur from the pre- to postwaiting period in either the clinic or home, providing support for the notion that the treatment program rather than the passage of time was responsible for the mother and child behavior change in the treatment group.

The PAT and the Becker Bipolar Adjective Checklist were also administered to the mothers in each group at the pre- and posttreatment assessments. In general, mothers in *both* groups perceived their children as better adjusted at post- than at pretreatment, suggesting that the changes in perceptions of the mothers in the treatment group did not result from treatment per se. This finding suggests that a parent perception measure alone may not be an adequate criterion upon which to base judgments concerning the effectiveness of parent training programs and again demonstrates the necessity of employing multiple outcome measures.

Generalization to the School Setting

The Peed *et al.* (1977) study provided convincing data concerning the immediate effectiveness of the training program in changing parent and child behavior in both the clinic and home. However, data were not provided concerning whether changes in child behaviors generalized from the clinic and home to the school setting. The effect of the treatment program on child behavior in the school as well as the home was of concern because Johnson, Bolstad, and Lobitz (1976) had reported data suggesting that children may increase their deviant behavior in school when deviant home behavior is treated by parent training programs. In order to determine whether such a "behavioral contrast" effect existed, or if setting generality (a decrease in deviant school behavior when noncompliance decreased in the home) occurred with our parent training program, two different investigations have been carried out.

In the first study, Forehand, Sturgis *et al.* (1979) measured the total amount of child deviant behavior in the school (e.g., crying, demanding attention, throwing tantrums, showing negativism) during observation sessions both before and after treatment for eight clinic-referred children. The standard home observational measures were also obtained for this group. In addition, the classroom deviant behavior of eight randomly selected "normal" school children was measured before and after a time interval that was equivalent to the one that separated the treated children's pre- and posttreatment measures. The results indicated that the expected changes in both parent and child behavior occurred in the home setting for the clinic group. In the school setting, three of the eight children treated for home noncompliance decreased their deviant school behavior and five increased such behavior from pre- to posttreatment assessments. For the randomly selected control children, four increased and four decreased their school deviant behavior. Statistical analysis of the data revealed no systematic changes in school behavior.

In a more recent study that employed a larger sample of 16 subjects, Breiner and Forehand (1981) utilized a similar design. In addition, they assessed both compliance and general deviant behavior in both the school and home settings. As in the earlier investigation, while the expected changes occurred in both parent and child behavior in the home setting, there were no significant changes in the children's classroom behavior in either a positive or negative direction. Thus, the results of these two studies indicate that treatment-induced changes in child behavior in the home are not associated with significant behavior change in the school (Mc-Mahon & Davies, 1980). Evidence for setting generality to the classroom was not generated by either study. However, these data also failed to support a behavioral contrast effect, since there were no systematic increases in deviant behavior in the classroom.

Temporal Generality (Maintenance)

At this point, our data indicated that the parenting program was immediately effective in changing parent and child behavior in both the clinic and home. However, the maintenance of these effects (i.e., temporal generality) was unknown. An additional experiment by Forehand, Sturgis et al. (1979) was undertaken to examine temporal generality resulting from the training program. The client sample consisted of 10 mother–child pairs, including the six mother–child pairs from the treatment group in the Peed et al. (1977) study. Data gathered in home observations that occurred both before and after treatment indicated that the subjects demonstrated pre- to posttreatment changes in the same parent and child behaviors as reported in the Peed et al. (1977) study. The temporal generality of the treatment program was assessed by means of data gathered from the 10 mother–child pairs at 6 and 12 months following treatment. Observations in the home revealed that the changes in mother and child behaviors observed immediately after treatment were maintained. An exception was the maternal use of contingent attention, which did not differ from the pretreatment level at the 6- and 12-month follow-ups. Mothers continued to report at both the 6- and 12-month follow-ups the positive attitude changes concerning their children (as measured by the PAT) that were evident immediately following treatment.

In a recent study, Baum and Forehand (in press) examined the long-term effectiveness of the parent training program by completing a follow-up assessment 1½ to 4½ years after treatment for 36 mother–child pairs. Thirty-four mothers completed the PAT and consumer satisfaction measures. Furthermore, 20 of the mothers and their children participated in home observations. The results indicated that child compliance and maternal perceptions of child adjustment changed significantly in the expected direction from pre- to posttreatment and remained at the posttreatment level at follow-up. Child deviant behavior decreased significantly from pre- to posttreatment and further decreased from posttreatment to follow-up. Positive parent behaviors improved from pre- to posttreatment. At follow-up these behaviors occurred significantly more frequently than at pretreatment, but significantly less frequently than at posttreatment. Maternal use of beta commands decreased from pre- to posttreatment and maintained at follow-up. Parent consumer satisfaction measures indicated that the parents were pleased with the treatment they had received.

Improvements in child behavior and parental perceptions of the child appear to be maintained following treatment. In addition, parents are satisfied with treatment up to 4½ years after their involvement in the program. Most parent behaviors, while still significantly improved from pretreatment levels, do not maintain at the level achieved during treatment. This finding is not surprising, as parents are encouraged initially to overuse the skills in order to facilitate their acquisition of the skills and to foster behavior change in their children.

Sibling Generality

Humphreys *et al.* (1978) examined the generality of treatment effects from one sibling to another. During four to eight pretreatment home observations and four posttreatment home observations, the interactions of the mother and clinic-referred child and of the mother and a sibling of the clinic-referred child were observed. In all eight cases, both the clinic-referred child and the sibling were 3 to 8 years old and the sibling was within 3 years of the clinic-referred child's age. During treatment the therapist did not discuss the application of the parenting techniques to the untreated sibling. If the mother initiated discussion of behavior problems in the untreated child, the therapist agreed that the procedures were general ones that were applicable to all children. No further elaboration of this point was made, and specific discussion of the sibling's behavior problems was deferred until after completion of the posttreatment observations.

The results indicated that from pre- to posttreatment the mothers significantly increased their use of attention contingent on compliance, rewards, and attends, and decreased their use of beta commands toward the untreated child. In addition, the untreated children increased their compliance. These results suggest that mothers can generalize their skills for dealing with noncompliance to other children in the family without the aid of direct programming by the therapist, and that the untreated children respond by increasing their compliance to maternal commands.

Behavioral Generality

In their review of the different types of generality, Forehand and Atkeson (1977) concluded that behavioral generality (i.e., change in behaviors not specifically targeted for treatment) had the least support in the parent training literature. For example, large-scale studies by Patterson and his colleagues (Patterson, 1974; Patterson et al., 1973; Patterson & Reid, 1973; Wiltz & Patterson, 1974) have all reported nonsignificant decreases in nontargeted deviant behaviors.

Of primary interest in examining behavioral generality in our parent training program was the relationship between a treated child behavior (noncompliance) and an untreated child behavior (other deviant behavior, which included tantrums, aggression, crying, etc.). Wells, Forehand, and Griest (1980) treated 12 noncompliant clinic-referred children and their mothers. Observational data of child behavior were collected from these families as well as from a nonclinic comparison group of 12 mother–child pairs. Mothers in the nonclinic group were selected from community volunteers who responded to announcements requesting participants for a research project, and whose children had no history of treatment for behavior problems. The clinic children significantly increased their compliance to both total and alpha commands from pre- to posttreatment, whereas the children in the nonclinic group did not change significantly on these measures. Further analysis indicated that the clinic and nonclinic groups differed significantly on both compliance measures at pre- but not at posttreatment. Most importantly, an examination of untreated child deviant behavior indicated that the clinic group decreased significantly from pre- to posttreatment on this measure and the nonclinic group did not change. The clinic group was significantly more deviant than the nonclinic group at pre- but not at posttreatment. These results provide evidence that generality from treated to untreated child behavior occurs with the parent training program and suggest that the successful treatment of noncompliance is sufficient in many cases to reduce other deviant behaviors that are not treated.

Social Validity

The use of a normative comparison group has also been employed in an assessment of the social validity of the parenting program (Forehand *et al.*, 1980). Based on Kazdin (1977) and Wolf (1978), four social validation procedures were employed: social comparison, subjective evaluation, social acceptability of treatment, and consumer satisfaction measures. Fifteen clinic-referred children and their mothers and 15 nonclinic children and their mothers served as subjects. Behavioral observations in the home setting were conducted pre- and posttreatment and at a 2-month follow-up for the clinic group and at comparable times for the nonclinic group. Parental questionnaires regarding their own adjustment (Beck Depression Inventory) and the adjustment of their children (PAT) were also completed before and after the treatment period and at the 2-month follow-up. Fifteen months after treatment consumer satisfaction and social acceptability of treatment measures were collected from parents in the clinic group. Only mothers in the clinic-referred group completed the parenting program.

The social comparison method of assessing social validity indicated that children in the clinic (treatment) group were less compliant and more deviant at pretreatment, but not at posttreatment or follow-up, than the nonclinic group. Thus, this method of social validation suggests that treatment had the desired outcome, since clinic-referred children were less compliant and more deviant prior to treatment, but not after treatment or at follow-up, than the nonclinic group. With respect to parental behaviors, mothers in the treatment group demonstrated a significant pre- to posttreatment improvement in positive attention as well as in command behavior. At posttreatment and follow-up, treatment-group mothers displayed more positive attention than the nonclinic group and similar levels of command behavior. There were also data to indicate that these behavioral improvements in both mother and child behavior were associated with improvements in self-report of maternal depression. Depression ratings improved significantly from pre- to posttreatment for mothers in the treatment group, and did not differ significantly from the nonclinic group at posttreatment or follow-up.

With respect to the subjective evaluation procedure, mothers in the treatment group reported significant improvement in their children's adjustment from pre- to posttreatment; however, they still perceived their children as less well adjusted than nonclinic mothers perceived their children at posttreatment. At the follow-up assessment, the two groups of mothers did not differ in their perceptions of their children's adjustment. This suggests that producing changes in maternal perceptions of child adjustment that are comparable to those held by mothers of nondeviant children may follow rather than accompany changes in child behavior.

On the social acceptability of treatment and consumer satisfaction measures collected 15 months after treatment termination, mothers in the treatment group indicated that they viewed the treatment procedures as being appropriate for dealing with their children's behavior problems. Furthermore, they reported that they were satisfied with treatment, they viewed their children as improved, they felt confident in managing their children, they viewed the therapists as being very helpful, and they frequently used the skills taught in the program.

The overall results of the Forehand *et al.* (1980) study, in conjunction with the normative comparisons of Wells, Forehand, and Griest (1980) in their investigation of behavioral generality, strongly suggest that the parenting program is a socially valid one.

ENHANCEMENT OF GENERALIZATION

Once the basic generality of the parenting program was established, our investigations shifted to the search for factors that might be involved in this process and ways in which we might enhance generalization and maintenance. Our attention has subsequently been focused on three rather different avenues of investigation: the addition of specific components to the basic treatment program, a self-help brochure, and the role of parental attitudes and personal adjustment. In this section, our work in each of these areas is described, and our findings to date summarized.

Additions to the Basic Parenting Program

Two investigations have been concerned with enhancing treatment outcome and generalization by means of a constructive treatment strategy (Kazdin, 1980). In this approach, components are added to a treatment package to make it more effective. In one study, the use of maternal self-control procedures was examined as a means of promoting temporal generalization of the effects of the parenting program (Wells, Griest, & Forehand, 1980). In the second investigation, McMahon, Forehand, and Griest (1981) examined the efficacy of incorporating formal training in social learning principles into the basic parenting program as a means of enhancing treatment outcome and generalization. Since the effectiveness and generality of the treatment program had been previously established, these studies were designed to focus on the *differential* effectiveness of incorporating additional treatment components into the parent training program.

Self-Control Training

The decision to incorporate a self-control strategy into the parenting program came about as a potential means of assisting the parent in maintaining the use of newly acquired parenting skills. As noted in Chapter 5, it has been suggested that improvements in child behavior and/or the reactions of others (spouses, relatives, etc.) may not provide sufficient reinforcement to maintain good parenting behavior (Conway & Bucher, 1976; Marholin *et al.*, 1976). Self-control procedures could conceivably circumvent these problems by providing a set of internally generated antecedent and consequent events necessary to control the parent's behavior, thereby reducing dependency on external reinforcement for the maintenance of treatment-acquired parenting skills.

Wells, Griest, and Forehand (1980) assigned 16 mothers and their clinic-referred noncompliant children to either a parent training alone group or a parent training plus self-control group. All mother–child pairs participated in the parenting program. As noted in Chapter 5, mothers in the combination group also learned to self-monitor their use of their new parenting skills and to reinforce themselves for the use of these skills during a 2-month follow-up period. The mother and therapist composed an individualized self-control program immediately after the posttreatment assessment. A list of self-reinforcers was compiled, and the mother entered into a contract with the therapist in which she agreed to practice the parenting skills with her child on a daily basis. Following each 15-minute "good parenting session," the mother administered one of these daily reinforcers to herself if she had provided positive attention to her child's appropriate behavior and provided the appropriate consequence for each occurrence of child noncompliance (TO). The mother was also encouraged to employ her treatment-acquired parenting skills as well as self-reinforcement strategies throughout the day.

Analyses of covariance using the pretreatment score as a covariate failed to find any differences between the two groups at posttreatment on observational measures of parent or child behavior. This finding was expected since the self-control manipulation occurred after the posttreatment observations. Of primary interest were analyses of differences between the two groups at follow-up as a function of the self-control contract followed by half of the mothers. Children in the parent training plus self-control group were significantly more compliant and less deviant than the children in the parent training alone group. No differences were obtained between groups on the observational measures of parent behavior (rewards plus attends, beta commands, contingent attention). This finding was unexpected, particularly given the differences obtained in child behavior and the fact that the primary focus of the self-control contract was on the parental behaviors of rewards plus attends and TO. In addition, it should be noted that two mothers in the self-control group did not actively participate in the self-control program. Thus, the results of this study provided evidence that self-control procedures may be of benefit to some mothers in the enhancement of temporal generality.

Training in Social Learning Principles

Another attempt to enhance the treatment outcome and generalization of our parenting program was reported by McMahon, Forehand, and Griest (1981). As noted in Chapter 5, one procedure that has been suggested as a potential means of enhancing generality is training parents in social learning principles in addition to basic behavioral parenting skills. Reasons for training parents in social learning principles have included the hypotheses that parents need the theoretical framework supplied by such principles, such training should allow subsequent performance of child management skills to accelerate more rapidly, and generalization is more likely to occur (O'Dell *et al.*, 1977; Patterson *et al.*, 1975). A number of parent training programs have incorporated such an approach into their treatment programs in varying degrees, while other programs have focused on training discrete behavioral skills. While it is apparent that investigators have recognized the potential importance of training parents in social learning principles, few data are available to suggest whether such training is beneficial, particularly in terms of enhancing generalization.

The McMahon, Forehand, and Griest (1981) study was designed to provide an analysis of the effectiveness of incorporating formal training in social learning principles into the parent training program as a means of enhancing treatment outcome and generalization. Twenty mother–child pairs who were referred for treatment of the child's behavior problems participated in the study. Each mother–child pair was assigned to one of two groups. The technique-alone parent training (TA) group received behavioral skill training via the treatment program. Therapists did not include any reference to, or explanations of, social learning principles in their

interactions with these parents.[1] The social learning parent training (SL) group also received training according to this format. In
addition, mothers in this group were given specific didactic instruction and brief reading assignments in various social learning
principles that were relevant to the parent training program, such
as characteristics of positive and negative reinforcement, shaping,
extinction, and punishment. Instruction in these principles was integrated into the program such that instruction preceded training of
a particular technique, but relevant points were repeated throughout the program as the skills were being applied.

Multiple outcome measures were used to assess temporal and
setting generality. As usual, home observational data were collected on both mother and child behavior, and the PAT was administered to assess maternal perceptions of child behavior. Additional
parent verbal report measures included the Knowledge of Behavioral Principles as Applied to Children (KBPAC) test (O'Dell et al.,
1979), which was administered to assess parental verbal understanding of basic social learning principles, and the Parent's Consumer
Satisfaction Questionnaire (PCSQ), which was administered to
assess the mothers' attitudes toward the particular treatment program they received. All but the PCSQ were collected prior to treatment, at the conclusion of treatment, and at a 2-month follow-up.
The consumer satisfaction scale was administered at the conclusion of treatment and at the follow-up.

Using the pretreatment score as the covariate, separate analyses of covariance were computed between groups on the posttreatment and follow-up scores for each dependent variable. At posttreatment and follow-up, mothers in the SL group demonstrated a
superior knowledge of social learning principles as measured by the
KBPAC compared to mothers in the TA group. This indicated

1. As noted earlier, the basic parent training program provides limited exposure to training in social learning principles. Thus, the TA group, while very
similar to the basic parent training program, was not identical to it.

that the experimental manipulation (i.e., training SL mothers in social learning principles) was effectively carried out. The results of the parent perception measure suggested that mothers in the SL group generally viewed their children in a more positive manner than did mothers in the TA group at both posttreatment and at follow-up.

The results of the observational measures of parent behavior indicated that mothers in the SL group emitted higher percentages of contingent attention than did TA mothers at either posttreatment or follow-up, as well as a higher frequency of attends plus rewards than TA mothers at follow-up. There were no differences between the groups with respect to frequency of beta commands at either posttreatment or follow-up. The observational measures of child behavior indicated that children in the SL group were significantly more compliant to maternal commands than were children in the TA group at the follow-up. There were no differences in compliance at posttreatment nor in deviant behavior at either posttreatment or follow-up between the two groups.

Mothers in both the SL and TA groups expressed a high level of overall satisfaction with their treatment program at both posttreatment and follow-up, as measured by the PCSQ. Mothers in the SL group tended to be more satisfied with their program at posttreatment than were TA mothers. Both groups reported similar levels of satisfaction at the follow-up.

In summary, the results of the McMahon, Forehand, and Griest (1981) study suggest that the integration of formal training in social learning principles into the parenting program enhanced treatment outcome, setting generality, and temporal generality.

Written Instructions as Self-Help Material

Another variation of our parenting program that has been experimentally validated is the use of a written brochure to teach parents to improve their nonclinic-referred children's mealtime behavior

(McMahon & Forehand, 1978). Three preschool-aged children and their mothers participated in the project. All were from middle-class families. Observations were conducted in the home by independent observers during mealtime (supper for two families, lunch for one). A multiple-baseline design across subjects was employed to assess the effects of the treatment brochure. Prior to baseline observations, each mother specified the mealtime behaviors she wished to modify from the Mealtime Behavior Checklist (see Chapter 5, Figure 5.2). Following the final baseline observation, the experimenter delivered the brochure to the mother. The brochure described the procedures of rewards and TO by presenting a short rationale for each technique, along with step-by-step instructions for their implementation, and examples of their use at mealtime (see Chapter 5). There was no therapist–client contact other than an initial interview to describe the project and the delivery of the brochure to the mothers after baseline, and there was no feedback given to the mothers at any point in the study. After baseline, observations continued in the home during mealtime for 7 to 16 days. Approximately 6 weeks following the final observation, five additional follow-up observations were carried out to assess maintenance.

Results indicated that inappropriate mealtime behavior decreased substantially for each child following introduction of the treatment brochure. The amount of reduction in these behaviors ranged from 50% to 80%. Furthermore, the changes were maintained for all three children at the follow-up observations. Maternal behavior also changed in the direction dictated by the brochure. Following introduction of the brochure, all three mothers substantially increased both rewards to their children's appropriate mealtime behavior and suitable responses to inappropriate mealtime behavior compared to baseline levels of response. At the 6-week follow-up, successful handling of inappropriate mealtime behavior continued to improve or remained at a level comparable to that during the intervention phase. Rewards for appropriate mealtime behavior declined from intervention phase levels at the follow-up; however, they still occurred more frequently than during the baseline. This uniform decline in the frequency of rewards was expected, as the mothers were instructed in the brochure to gradually thin the schedule of reinforcement. The degree of change manifested by these mothers was comparable to results obtained in the basic parent training program with clinic-referred children utilizing therapist instruction, modeling, and feedback (Peed *et al.*, 1977). Thus, this study indicates that written instructions alone can effectively prompt mothers to modify their children's inappropriate mealtime behavior in the home setting, and that these changes maintain for at least 6 weeks. Written instructions for this particular problem behavior may be considered for use alone or in conjunction with the standard parent training program.

Parental Attitudes and Personal Adjustment

A pair of studies relating to client characteristics associated with completion of the parenting program and subsequent follow-up assessments were indirect indicators that parental personal adjustment might be an important factor in the generalization of treatment effects. In the first study (McMahon, Forehand, Griest, & Wells, 1981), 48 mother–child pairs who had been referred to our clinic were assessed prior to treatment on demographic variables (sex and age of the child and socioeconomic status of the family), a measure of parent adjustment (the Beck Depression Inventory), three parent perception measures of child adjustment (PAT: Home Attitude, Behavior Rating, and Adjective Checklist Scales), two measures of child behavior (child compliance to parental commands and child inappropriate behavior), and two measures of parent behavior (rewards and commands). Eight of the 48 mothers dropped out of treatment. Two dropped out prior to attending any treatment session, three after one session, two after two sessions, and one after five sessions. Analyses of variance indicated that the dropout group was significantly lower in socioeconomic status, was more depressed, and issued more commands than the group that completed treatment. In a subsequent investigation, Griest, Forehand, and Wells (in press) examined client characteristics associated with participation in follow-up assessments of the effects of the parenting program. Using similar measures they found the maternal depression at the pretreatment assessment was again associated with an increased probability that the mother would refuse to participate in these follow-up assessments. These data suggest that for at least some clinic-referred mothers, pre-existing depression might influence participation in various activities associated with positive therapeutic outcome.

Stronger evidence supporting the role of maternal depression in parent–child interactions comes from data collected by Griest, Wells, and Forehand (1979). Parental perception of the child's adjustment has consistently been the most reliable indicator of clinic versus nonclinic status (Lobitz & Johnson, 1975). Since there is evidence in the depression literature to suggest that depression can affect the individual's perception of external events (Beck, 1967; Kovacs & Beck, 1978), the purpose of this study was to examine the relative contributions of maternal depression and child behavior to maternal perceptions of their clinic-referred children.

Stepwise multiple regression analyses were performed on data collected from 22 mother–child pairs referred to our clinic. Maternal depression (as measured by the Beck Depression Inventory), child compliance, and other deviant child behavior served as predictor variables, and each of the three scales of a parent perception measure (the PAT) served as the criterion variable. For each of the three criterion variables, the mother's depression score on the Beck was the first variable selected for inclusion in the regression analysis, indicating it was the best predictor. There was a significant positive relationship between depression scores and maternal perceptions of their children on two of the three criterion measures (Behavior Rating and Adjective Checklist Scales), demonstrating that the more depressed mothers perceived their children as more malad-justed. Neither child compliance nor child deviant behavior contributed significantly to any of the three regression analyses. Thus, this study suggests that factors other than the child's behavior may account for maternal perceptions of the child's adjustment. One of these factors appears to be maternal depression.

A more comprehensive assessment of the role of predictors of maternal perceptions of the child's adjustment was subsequently undertaken utilizing both clinic-referred and nonclinic subjects (Griest et al., 1980). Prior research, which has attempted to identify differences in parent-child interactions between clinic-referred and nonclinic children, has examined four factors: child behavior, parent behavior, parent perceptions of child behavior, and parental personal adjustment. However, these four factors had not been examined in a systematic and comprehensive manner.

There were 20 mother-child pairs in both the clinic and nonclinic groups. The groups were matched on a number of demographic variables, including sex and age of the child, socioeconomic status of the family, mother's marital status, and race. Measures included child and parent behavior recorded by home observers, mother-recorded rates of child behavior, maternal perceptions of the child's behavior (three scales from the PAT and three scales from the Becker Bipolar Adjective Checklist), and personal adjustment of the mother. With respect to this latter dimension, the Beck Depression Inventory was used to rate levels of maternal depression, the modified form of Locke's Marital Adjustment Test allowed mothers to rate their marital satisfaction, and the trait form of the State-Trait Anxiety Inventory (Spielberger, Gorsuch, & Lushene, 1970) was administered to obtain ratings of maternal anxiety.

The clinic and nonclinic groups differed on a number of dimensions. Clinic children were significantly less compliant (as measured by both an independent observer and by the mother) and were perceived by their mothers as significantly more maladjusted (on all six parent perception measures) than were nonclinic children. With respect to maternal self-report of personal adjustment, clinic mothers judged themselves to be significantly more depressed and anxious that nonclinic mothers.

A stepwise discriminant analysis of the outcome measures was performed to determine which variables, both singly and in combination, were the best predictors of clinic–nonclinic status. The six maternal perception measures of child behavior each accounted for 46% to 57% of the predictive variance individually. A combination of four of these parent perception measures (Behavior Rating and Adjective Checklist Scales from the PAT and the More Conduct Problems and Less Withdrawn and Hostile scales from the Becker) accounted for 77% of the variance between the groups. The next best individual and combined predictors of group membership accounted for substantially less of the variance.

Since the maternal perception measures of child behavior were the best discriminators between the groups, multiple regression analyses were conducted separately with the clinic and nonclinic groups to examine whether child behavior or maternal adjustment best predicted parental perceptions of their children in each group. For the nonclinic group, maternal perceptions of child adjustment were best predicted by the child's behavior, whereas for the clinic group, maternal perceptions of child adjustment were best predicted by an interaction of child behavior and the mother's personal adjustment (as measured by the State–Trait Anxiety Inventory, trait form). Thus, these results suggest that a complex interaction of factors is occurring in clinic families that is not present in nonclinic families. This interaction of child behavior and maternal adjustment appears to be one critical factor that determines whether mothers will perceive their children as being in need of psychological services. It should be noted that the exact etiology of this interaction cannot be determined from the present data. Maladjusted mothers may exert a significant influence on the occurrence of behavior problems of their children, the children's behavior may cause the mothers' maladjustment, or the etiology may be due to some unidentified third factor.

An additional study has recently been conducted in an attempt to identify and examine differences in parent characteristics between two clinic-referred subgroups of children (Rickard, Forehand, Wells, Griest, & McMahon, 1981). Children in the clinic deviant group were significantly more noncompliant and deviant than a nonclinic sample. On the other hand, children in the clinic nondeviant group, although referred for noncompliance and other behavior problems, did not differ from a nonclinic sample on either of these behaviors. It was hypothesized that mothers in both clinic-referred groups would perceive their children as more deviant than mothers of nonclinic children perceived their children. However, it was also hypothesized that the mothers in the clinic deviant group would lack appropriate parenting skills, while the mothers in the clinic nondeviant group would be more depressed than the nonclinic sample or the clinic deviant sample. These predictions were based on the assumption that the clinic deviant children were referred because they actually were more deviant and noncompliant than the nonclinic and clinic nondeviant children. The greater deviance and noncompliance by the clinic deviant group of children might be expected to result from ineffective parenting skills in this group. In contrast, the clinic nondeviant group was hypothesized to have been referred because of maternal adjustment problems that affected maternal perception of the child's adjustment.

Home observations by independent observers and parent questionnaries examining parental adjustment (the Beck Depression Inventory) and parental perceptions of child adjustment (the PAT) were completed. Results indicated that both clinic groups perceived their children as more maladjusted than parents in the nonclinic group perceived their children, thus replicating the findings of Griest et al. (1980) and others (Lobitz & Johnson, 1975).

More importantly, the other experimental hypotheses were supported. Mothers of the children in the clinic nondeviant group were significantly more depressed than those in the remaining two groups. Since the children in the clinic nondeviant group were not more deviant or noncompliant than the nonclinic group, it appears that the mothers' personal adjustment (in this case, depression) rather than the children's behavior was a significant factor in the referral of these children for treatment (see Griest *et al.*, 1979). An additional finding was that mothers in the clinic deviant group issued more beta commands than did mothers in the clinic nondeviant group, supporting the hypothesis that the deviant behavior of these children was associated with ineffective parenting skills.

CONCLUSIONS

In this chapter, we have attempted to present a thorough yet relatively concise summary of the many investigations concerning the effects of the parent training program that we have conducted over the past 9 years. The earlier studies were designed to specify relevant variables and parameters of these variables for inclusion in the program. The importance of parental use of social reinforcement, appropriate commanding, and TO was demonstrated. In two initial evaluations of the treatment package, it was found that the program is associated with changes in parent and child behavior in the clinic setting. The initial studies on generalization were designed to assess the various types of generality of treatment effects. Briefly, these studies indicated that setting (to the home), temporal, sibling, and behavioral generality occurred. The social validity of the parenting program was also demonstrated, since maternal and child behavior, as well as maternal personal adjustment and perceptions of child adjustment, were within normal limits following treatment or at follow-up. One limitation of the program's effectiveness was also demonstrated by these studies.

There is no consistent evidence of setting generality to the school, but neither is there evidence of a behavioral contrast effect in the classroom. Clinicians would do well to assess child behavior in the classroom when parent training is undertaken so that a separate intervention may be developed in that setting if necessary.

More recent studies have been concerned with ways to enhance generalization and to examine more basic factors that might be involved in the generalization process. Additions to the basic parenting program have included a maternal self-control component and the integration of training in social learning principles. Self-control procedures appear to enhance positive child behavior; however, more research is needed to determine which mothers are most likely to employ, and benefit from, such an approach. Training mothers in social learning principles resulted in a greater enhancement of treatment outcome as well as temporal and setting generality. Of particular interest may be the finding that this component enhanced maternal perceptions of the child.

We have also found that written instructions can be used in a self-administered fashion by mothers to improve their children's inappropriate mealtime behavior, and that these positive changes in both mother and child behavior are maintained. An area of future research involves more extensive evaluation of this approach to parent training, using different types of brochures and extending the investigations to include clinic-referred as well as nonclinic-referred children and parents.

Finally, a series of investigations concerning the role of maternal adjustment as a contributing factor in generalization were carried out. These studies have indicated that mothers of nonclinic (i.e., "normal") children base their perceptions of their children's adjustment on the children's behavior; that is, they are more accurate interpreters of the children's behavior. In addition, they are less anxious and depressed than mothers of clinic-referred children. The more negative perceptions of the mothers of clinic-referred children, on the other hand, are influenced by a combination of the children's behavior and the mothers' own level of personal adjustment. Not only is this higher level of personal maladjustment associated with a more negative perception of their children, but lower levels of self-reported personal adjustment (e.g., depression) are also associated with failing to complete the parenting program or to participate in follow-up assessments at a later time. A recent investigation suggests that there are at least two identifiable subgroups of mothers of clinic-referred children: those with a deficit in parenting skills per se (and whose children are more deviant than nonclinic children), and mothers who are experiencing personal adjustment problems but whose children are no more deviant than nonclinic children.

These studies suggest a number of important steps that should be taken as a potential means of enhancing the effectiveness of the parent training program. First, it is quite obvious that parental adjustment as well as child adjustment, child behavior, and parent behavior must be assessed when these families are referred for professional assistance. Our assessment of maternal personal adjustment, although limited to self-report measures of depression, anxiety, and/or marital satisfaction, has indicated the importance of this aspect for at least some mothers. In some cases, treatment may need to focus on the parent's maladjustment rather than, or in addition to, the remediation of ineffective parenting skills. Finally, it is clear that adequate normative data for both child behavior and parent behavior, perceptions, and personal adjustment are necessary to determine if treatment is necessary, and, if so, where that treatment should be focused (e.g., parental personal adjustment and/or parenting skills).

In conclusion, we believe that our investigations have contributed to the alleviation of parent–child conflict, and that our work has facilitated the maintenance and generalization of these positive effects. More importantly, we sincerely hope that we have been able to enrich the lives of parents and children in a meaningful way.

APPENDIX A.
PARENT'S CONSUMER
SATISFACTION
QUESTIONNAIRE

Parent's Name _____   Date _____

The following questionnaire is part of our evaluation of the treatment program that you have received. It is important that you answer as honestly as possible. The information obtained will help us to evaluate and continually improve the program we offer. Your cooperation is greatly appreciated.

A. The Overall Program

Please circle the response that best expresses how you honestly feel.

1. The major problem(s) that originally prompted me to begin treatment for my child is (are) at this point

considerably   worse   slightly   the   slightly   improved   greatly
  worse   worse   same   improved   improved

2. My child's problems that have been treated at the clinic are at this point

considerably   worse   slightly   the   slightly   improved   greatly
  worse   worse   same   improved   improved

3. My child's problems that have *not* been treated at the clinic are

| considerably worse | worse | slightly worse | the same | slightly improved | improved | greatly improved |

4. My feelings at this point about my child's progress are that I am

| very dissatisfied | dissatisfied | slightly dissatisfied | neutral | slightly satisfied | satisfied | very satisfied |

5. To what degree has the treatment program helped with other general personal or family problems not directly related to your child?

| hindered much more than helped | hindered | hindered slightly | neither helped nor hindered | helped slightly | helped | helped very much |

6. At this point, my expectation for a satisfactory outcome of the treatment is

| very pessimistic | pessimistic | slightly pessimistic | neutral | slightly optimistic | optimistic | very optimistic |

7. I feel the approach to treating my child's behavior problems in the home by using this type of parent training program is

| very inappropriate | inappropriate | slightly inappropriate | neutral | slightly appropriate | appropriate | very appropriate |

8. Would you recommend the program to a friend or relative?

| strongly recommend | recommend | slightly recommend | neutral | slightly not recommend | not recommend | strongly not recommend |

9. How confident are you in managing *current* behavior problems in the home on your own?

| very confident | confident | somewhat confident | neutral | somewhat unconfident | unconfident | very unconfident |

10. How confident are you in your ability to manage *future* behavior problems in the home using what you learned from this program?

| very unconfident | unconfident | somewhat unconfident | neutral | somewhat confident | confident | very confident |

11. My overall feeling about the treatment program for my child and family is

| very negative | negative | somewhat negative | neutral | slightly positive | positive | very positive |

B. Teaching Format

Difficulty

In this section, we'd like to get your ideas of how difficult each of the following types of teaching has been for you to follow. Please circle the response that most closely describes your opinion.

1. Lecture information

| extremely easy | easy | somewhat easy | neutral | somewhat difficult | difficult | extremely difficult |

2. Demonstration of skills by the therapist

| extremely easy | easy | somewhat easy | neutral | somewhat difficult | difficult | extremely difficult |

3. Practice of skills in the clinic with the therapist

| extremely easy | easy | somewhat easy | neutral | somewhat difficult | difficult | extremely difficult |

4. Practice of skills in the clinic with your child

| extremely easy | easy | somewhat easy | neutral | somewhat difficult | difficult | extremely difficult |

5. Practicing the Child's Game at home

| extremely easy | easy | somewhat easy | neutral | somewhat difficult | difficult | extremely difficult |

6. Other homework assignments

| extremely easy | easy | somewhat easy | neutral | somewhat difficult | difficult | extremely difficult |

7. The written materials you were asked to read

| extremely easy | easy | somewhat easy | neutral | somewhat difficult | difficult | extremely difficult |

Usefulness

In this section, we'd like to get your ideas of how useful each of the following types of teaching is for you *now*. Please circle the response that most clearly describes your opinion.

1. Lecture information

| extremely not useful | not useful | somewhat not useful | neutral | somewhat useful | useful | extremely useful |

2. Demonstration of skills by the therapist

extremely not useful	not useful	somewhat not useful	neutral	somewhat useful	useful	extremely useful

3. Practice of skills in the clinic with the therapist

extremely not useful	not useful	somewhat not useful	neutral	somewhat useful	useful	extremely useful

4. Practice of skills in the clinic with your child

extremely not useful	not useful	somewhat not useful	neutral	somewhat useful	useful	extremely useful

5. Practicing the Child's Game at home

extremely not useful	not useful	somewhat not useful	neutral	somewhat useful	useful	extremely useful

6. Other homework assignments

extremely not useful	not useful	somewhat not useful	neutral	somewhat useful	useful	extremely useful

7. The written materials you were asked to read

extremely not useful	not useful	somewhat not useful	neutral	somewhat useful	useful	extremely useful

C. Specific Parenting Techniques

Difficulty

In this section we'd like to get your idea of how difficult it usually is to do each of the following techniques *now*. Please circle the response that most closely describes how difficult the technique is to do.

1. Attends

extremely easy	easy	somewhat easy	neutral	somewhat difficult	difficult	extremely difficult

2. Rewards

extremely easy	easy	somewhat easy	neutral	somewhat difficult	difficult	extremely difficult

3. Ignoring

extremely easy	easy	somewhat easy	neutral	somewhat difficult	difficult	extremely difficult

4. Good (alpha) commands

extremely easy	easy	somewhat easy	neutral	somewhat difficult	difficult	extremely difficult

5. Time-out

extremely easy	easy	somewhat easy	neutral	somewhat difficult	difficult	extremely difficult

6. The overall group of techniques

extremely easy	easy	somewhat easy	neutral	somewhat difficult	difficult	extremely difficult

Usefulness

In this section, we'd like to have your opinion of how useful each of the following techniques is to you in improving your interaction with your child and decreasing his or her "bad" behavior *now*. Please circle the response that most closely describes the usefulness of the technique.

1. Attends

extremely not useful	not useful	somewhat not useful	neutral	somewhat useful	useful	extremely useful

2. Rewards

extremely not useful	not useful	somewhat not useful	neutral	somewhat useful	useful	extremely useful

3. Ignoring

extremely not useful	not useful	somewhat not useful	neutral	somewhat useful	useful	extremely useful

4. Good (alpha) commands

extremely not useful	not useful	somewhat not useful	neutral	somewhat useful	useful	extremely useful

5. Time-out

extremely not useful	not useful	somewhat not useful	neutral	somewhat useful	useful	extremely useful

6. The overall group of techniques

extremely not useful	not useful	somewhat not useful	neutral	somewhat useful	useful	extremely useful

D. Therapist(s)

In this section we'd like to get your ideas about your therapist(s). Please circle the response to each question that best expresses how you feel.

1. I feel that the therapist's teaching was

very poor	fair	slightly below average	average	slightly above average	high	superior

2. The therapist's preparation was

poor	fair	slightly below average	average	slightly above average	high	superior

3. Concerning the therapist's interest and concern in me and my problems with my child, I was

extremely dissatisfied	dissatisfied	slightly dissatisfied	neutral	slightly satisfied	satisfied	extremely satisfied

4. At this point, I feel that the therapist in the treatment program was

extremely not helpful	not helpful	slightly not helpful	neutral	slightly helpful	helpful	extremely helpful

5. Concerning my personal feelings toward the therapist

I dislike him/her very much	I dislike him/her	I dislike him/her slightly	I have a neutral attitude toward him/her	I like him/her slightly	I like him/her	I like him/her very much

E. Your Opinion Please

1. What part of the program was most helpful to you?

2. What did you like most about the program?

3. What did you like least about the program?

4. What part of the program was least helpful to you?

5. How could the program have been improved to help you more?

Thank you. Now please enclose this questionnaire in the attached envelope and drop it in the mail.

SCORING INSTRUCTIONS

Score all items on a 7-point scale.

A. Overall Program
   Items 1, 2, 3, 4, 5, 6, 7, 10, and 11 are scored on a 1- to 7-point scale (i.e., if first answer is circled, the item is assigned a point value of 1, if second answer is circled, the item is assigned a point value of 2, etc.), while items 8 and 9 are scored on a 7- to 1-point scale.

B. Teaching Format
   Difficulty: Score all items on a 1- to 7-point scale.
   Usefulness: Score all items on a 1- to 7-point scale.
C. Specific Parenting Techniques
   Difficulty: Score all items on a 1- to 7-point scale.
   Usefulness: Score all items on a 1- to 7-point scale.
D. Therapist(s)
   Score all items on a 1- to 7-point scale.

APPENDIX B.
BEHAVIORAL
CODING SYSTEM

THE SCORE SHEET

EXAMPLE:

Each score sheet contains 10 rectangular blocks, subdivided into three rows and 10 columns, with a circle following each rectangle (see example above and the blank score sheet at the end of Appendix B, p. 218). Each rectangle represents 30 seconds of observation time. The three rows represent three categories of behavior: parental antecedents in row 1, child responses in row 2, and parental consequences in row 3. The behaviors recorded within a single column indicate a sequence of related behaviors or an interaction. The columns also denote the order of occurrence for these interactions. They do not provide precise temporal information since the time span represented between columns may range from 1 to 29 seconds. Note that up to 10 interactions may be scored each 30 seconds (1 per column); all subsequent interactions in the 30-second interval are not scored. Most often, however, fewer than 10 columns will be used, since fewer than 10 interactions will occur in 30 seconds. Also, in most cases not all rows in each column will be used. From one to three rows per column may be used, contingent on the interaction that occurs. In summary, each rectangle marks a 30-second interval, each row indicates a different category of behavior, and each column contains an interaction consisting of a sequence of one to three behaviors.

The circle on the score sheet will be used to record an additional category of child behavior on an interval sampling basis. The category to be coded is that of appropriateness of child behavior. Each circle will be scored for the same 30-second interval as the rectangle that precedes it. Inappropriate child behavior will be recorded at the time that behavior occurs during the 30-second interval. However, inappropriate child behavior may be recorded only once per circle regardless of subsequent occurrences during the remainder of the interval. If child behavior is appropriate for the entire 30-second interval, appropriate child behavior will be recorded in the circle. Therefore, the circle will essentially denote the presence or absence of at least one inappropriate behavior.

During observations, an audiotape will cue observers at the end of each 30-second interval to shift to the next rectangle and circle.

THE OBSERVATION SETTING

When observing in the home, each observer will obtain 40 minutes (80 rectangular units or 8 coding sheets) of observation data per session. Each parent and child will participate in blocks of four home observation sessions before and after the treatment program. Only one observation session will occur per day. Ideally, observations will occur on successive days. The following conditions will be maintained during observation sessions:

1. Parent and child must remain in two rooms (one room if visibility is restricted).
2. Parent and child may bring any work materials or toys desired into the observation area, with the exception of commercial board games (e.g., Candyland, Monopoly) or playing cards.
3. Television watching is prohibited.
4. The parent is not to read stories to the child.
5. The child should not have friends over during observation sessions; other siblings may be present but this should remain consistent across observations. The other parent (who is not being

observed), relatives, or other visitors should not be present ordinarily during the observation period. On some occasions, both parents' interactions (with the child) may be coded either on an alternating 5-minute basis or by conducting separate observation sessions with each parent and the child.

6. The parent is encouraged to answer telephone calls briefly or to return the calls later in the day.

7. If the parent leaves the observation area (or is talking on the telephone), the audiotape is stopped until the parent returns. Coding resumes at that point, even if it is in the middle of an interval.

8. If the child leaves the observation area, scoring continues as long as the parent is visible and is attempting to get the child to return. If the parent gives up this effort, recording is stopped and the parent is prompted to bring the child back. When the child is in time-out (TO), continue scoring even if the TO area is not within the observation area. (It may be somewhat difficult in these situations to hear and/or see the interaction.)

9. If the child leaves to go to the bathroom, recording stops. It is suggested to the parent that this need occur only once per session. The recommended policy is to have the parent check on the child's bathroom needs prior to the observation session.

10. All requests for therapy information are referred to the therapist. Under no circumstances are observers to give any advice or suggestions on how to manage children.

11. If the parent asks what the observer is writing during the observation, the observer is to say something to the effect of "This is a code of things that are going on. If I explained it now, I'd probably just confuse you. The therapist will be telling you more about it as you go along."

12. The observer should record questions, comments, suggestions, or unusual occurrences during the observation in the margin of the coding sheet. However, this should not interfere with observation of the parent–child interaction.

THE CATEGORIES: SYMBOLS AND RULES OF SCORING

The category of appropriateness of child behavior is recorded in the circles and consists of the following behaviors:

Category	Symbol	Behavior
1. Appropriateness of child behavior	✔	1. Inappropriate child behavior
		a. Whining, crying, yelling, tantrums
		b. Aggression
		c. Deviant talk
	0	2. Appropriate child behavior

Listed below are the three categories of behavior recorded in the three rows of the rectangles and the behaviors included in each category.

Category	Symbol	Behavior
1. Parental antecedents (row 1)	C	1. Command
	W	2. Warning
	Q	3. Question
	A	4. Attend
	R	5. Reward
2. Child responses (row 2)	C	1. Compliance
	N	2. Noncompliance
3. Parental consequences (row 3)	A	1. Attend
	R	2. Reward

There is an additional parental consequence that is scored. This is the implementation of a time-out (TO) procedure.

Examine the sample score sheet, Figure B.1. Notice that all circles have been scored as either appropriate or inappropriate child behavior. All circles must always be scored. The rule for scoring inappropriate child behavior (✔) is simply that at least one of the three forms of inappropriate behavior occurred at some point during the interval. Inappropriate behavior is scored at the time it occurs. Appropriate child behavior may be scored only at the end of a 30-second interval. Appropriate behavior (0) is the absence of any inappropriate behavior during an entire interval.

Notice two points about the rectangles. First, within any given rectangle all of the columns are not scored. As noted previously, only rarely will 10 or more scorable behavioral interactions occur during a 30-second interval. Second, all three categories (rows) in the rectangle need not be scored in any given interaction (column). The following rules determine what categories of behavior are scored for any given interaction.

1. The occurrence of any of the five parental antecedents (category 1) is recorded in row 1, unless all 10 columns in the rectangle have been used before the 30-second interval is completed. Parental antecedents are recorded in order beginning in the far left column. A parental antecedent is the cue that initiates the start of an interaction.
2. A child response (category 2) may be scored in row 2 if and only if the recorded parental antecedent in row 1 was a command (C) or a warning (W). If a child response does not occur, the next recording will be a parental antecedent placed in row 1 of the next column to the right.
3. A parental consequence (category 3) may be scored in row 3 if and only if the recorded child response in row 2 was compliance (C). If the child response was noncompliance (N), the next scoring will again be a parental antecedent in row 1 of the next column (unless TO is initiated).
4. TO is scored in row 3 or below the rectangle, depending upon how the parent implements the procedure.

To summarize, the rules for scoring an interaction or sequence of behaviors specify that any recordable parental antecedent, up to 10 per rectangle, is always scored. A score for category 2 (child responses) depends on the occurrence of a specific type of parental antecedent (C or W) in category 1. A score for category 3 (parental consequences) depends on the occurrence of a specific child response (C) in category 2. TO may be scored in either row 3 or in the margin below the rectangle.

DEFINITIONS OF BEHAVIOR AND EXAMPLES OF SCORING

Appropriateness of Child Behavior

An interval sampling procedure is used to record these behaviors in the circles. Interval sampling requires a binary decision by the coder: Either the child's behavior is appropriate for the entire 30-second interval, or the child emits one or more of the three forms of inappropriate behavior listed below. Immediately after one of the inappropriate behaviors is

SCORE SHEET

Child's Name __Begood,_____Jack_____
Date __9/17/81__ Last _____ Time __5:30__ First
Coder's Name _____JKL_____
Session ____1_____ Place __HOME_____

1

C	C	A	C	C					
		N	C						

O

2

A	A	C	C	Q	C				
					C				

O

3

C	C	Q	Q	C̄	C̄				
				C					

✓

4

R	C	C	C	Q					
			N						

✓

5

C	C	Q	A	C	C	W			
C				N					
				TO					

O

6

✓

7

O

8

⧄	C	C	Q						

O

9

Q	A	Q	C	C	W				
			C		N				
			R		TO⧄				

O

10

C	C	Q	Q						

✓

ROW 1	ROW 2	ROW 3	CIRCLE	OTHER
C command	C compliance	A attend	✓ inappropriate child beh.	TO time-out
W warning	N noncompliance	R reward	O appropriate child beh.	
Q question				
A attend				
R reward				

188

observed, record a checkmark (ν) in the circle being coded. Disregard further inappropriate acts occurring within that interval. In the absence of inappropriate child behavior, place a zero (0) in the circle.

Inappropriate Child Behavior

1. *Whining, crying, yelling, tantrums.* Crying and yelling are self-explanatory. Whining includes the following situations: (a) whines over minor injuries or threats; (b) nags the parent in order to get something done; (c) seeks attention by whining; (d) whines when parent leaves. Tantrums are any combination of whining, yelling, crying, hitting, and kicking. All of these are to be scored as inappropriate, regardless of the eliciting situation.

2. *Aggression.* This includes behaviors in which the child damages or destroys an object or attempts or threatens to damage an object or injure a person. The potential for damage to objects or injury to persons is the critical factor in scoring, not the actual occurrence. It is usually not scored as deviant if it is appropriate within the context of the play situation (e.g., ramming cars in a car crash). Examples of aggression toward persons include biting, kicking, slapping, hitting, or grabbing an object roughly away from another person, or threatening to do any of the preceding.

3. *Deviant talk.* This encompasses all inappropriate child verbal behavior, including repetitive requests for attention (at least three requests occurring one right after the other); stated refusals to comply (not the *act* of noncompliance); disrespectful (sassy) statements; profanity; and commands to parents that threaten aversive consequences.

EXAMPLES OF REPETITIVE REQUESTS:

CHILD: "Can I go outside now? Can I? Huh, Daddy, huh?"
CHILD: "Look at me, Mommy! Mommy! Look, Mommy!"

EXAMPLES OF STATED REFUSALS TO COMPLY:

CHILD: "I won't put my toys away."
CHILD: "I don't need a bath and you can't make me take one."

FIG. B.1. SAMPLE SCORE SHEET

CHILD: "I'll go to bed when I want, not when you say."

EXAMPLES OF DISRESPECTFUL STATEMENTS:

CHILD: "You're just an old fatso!"
CHILD: "You're mean to me and I don't like you anymore."

EXAMPLES OF PROFANITY:

CHILD: "I don't give a damn about this game."
CHILD: "Oh, hell!"

EXAMPLES OF THREATENING COMMANDS:

CHILD: "You leave me alone or I'll scream."
CHILD: "I'm going to get mad at you, Mommy, if you tell me to do one more thing."

Appropriate Child Behavior

Appropriate child behavior is defined as the absence of all inappropriate behaviors listed above. Note that since an interval sampling procedure is used for this category, behavior must be appropriate for the entire interval for appropriate behavior to be recorded.

Parental Antecedents (Category 1)

The five parent behaviors outlined below initiate the recording of behavioral interactions (columns) and are, therefore, the building blocks of all coding done in the rectangles. With one exception (physical rewards), all behaviors are verbal. Although a behavior may have several "forms," all forms of a behavior are scored as if identical. The five behaviors are mutually exclusive. Particularly difficult discriminations for each behavior are presented and critical factors for making discriminations are discussed.

Only parental behaviors directed to or including the target child are scored. The two major instances where this is a factor are the parental use of "we" and when there are other children in the observation area in addition to the target child.

EXAMPLES:

PARENT: "We need some more toys." (C)
PARENT: "I need some more toys." (not scored)
PARENT: "I think we need some more toys." (C)
PARENT: (target child playing with blocks, sister coloring) "That's a pretty picture." (not scored)
PARENT: (target child playing with blocks, sister coloring) "You're playing quietly." (A)

Command (C): Alpha

There are two basic classes of commands: alpha and beta. Although each class is defined differently, both are scored as commands (C) in row 1. For the sake of clarity, alpha and beta commands are presented separately here. An alpha command is an order, suggestion, question, rule, or contingency to which a motoric or verbal response is appropriate and feasible. In question commands, a motoric response must be available. The following are the various types of alpha commands.

1. *Direct commands.* Orders that are stated directly and specify the child behavior to be initiated or inhibited are direct commands.

EXAMPLES:

"Play with the blocks."
"Look here."
"Come here."
"Build it higher."
"Find another one."
"Color it red."
"Tell your sister about it."
"Say 'elephant' for Mommy."
"Roll it into a ball."
"Put it below the line."
"Stop kicking me."
"Do not do that."
"Be quiet."
"No."
"Let me put the block on the tower."

2. *Indirect commands.* Suggestions to respond motorically or verbally that are not in question form are indirect commands.

EXAMPLES:

"Let's play cowboys."
"See if you can be quiet."
"Let's don't do that anymore, please."
"Maybe you can tell me the answer."
"You should pick up the toys now."

3. *Question commands.* Questions to which a motoric response is available in addition to the verbal response and that *direct* the child's behavior as opposed to following it constitute question commands.

EXAMPLES:

"Why don't you make it higher?"
"Can you tell me what color this is?"
"Could you draw me a picture?"
"Can you add some more to it?"
"Wouldn't it be nice to play with the baby?"
"Shouldn't you roll it up more?"
"Why don't we sit here?"
"Hand me the car, will you?"
"Are you going to color it red?"

It is important to note that in order to be scored as a C, the question must *direct* the child's behavior as opposed to following the child's behavior (the latter would be scored as a Q).

EXAMPLES:

PARENT: (child coloring in book) "Are you going to keep coloring?" (C, because child is to continue the activity)
PARENT: "Are you coloring?" (Q, follows child's activity)
PARENT: (child sitting on floor) "Are you going to color?" (C)
PARENT: (child coloring in book) "Are you going to color?" (Q)

There is one exception to the rules stated above for scoring a question command as a command. Questions beginning with "Do you want . . . " are *always* scored as a question (Q) and never as a command (C).

4. *Permission statements and rules.* Permission statements ("You may . . . ") or rules ("There will be . . . ") are those that specify a behavior to be initiated or inhibited in the present.

EXAMPLES:

"There will be no more fighting."
"You may play with the blocks now."
"There should be no loud talking while I'm reading."
"You may not play near the lamp."
"There is to be no fussing now while the baby is asleep."
"We are going to build a house now."
"You can make it higher."

5. *If . . . then statements.* These are contingency statements that do not qualify as warnings because the "then" component refers to a positive or neutral consequence or a negative event *not* administered by either parent. Thus, the "if . . . " part of the phrase is the command, while the "then . . . " component is simply information that is not scored. At times, the statement may be verbalized as "then . . . if." This does not affect the scoring. Note that when the consequent (or "then . . . ") component suggests an aversive event to be administered by either parent, the entire "if . . . then" statement is scored as a warning (W).

EXAMPLES:

"If you don't be quiet, you'll wake the baby."
"If you're real good, I'll give you some cookies."
"If you put on one more, it will all fall down."
"Suzy will get mad if you don't leave her alone."
"I'll be so proud of you if you get that all cleaned up."
"If you don't stop running, you'll hurt yourself."
"If you hit your sister again, I will send you to your room." (W)

6. *Chain commands.* Chain commands are a series of logically or

syntactically related commands that are given in rapid succession without pause (thereby forming a single unit of speech). In nearly all cases, the cue for scoring two or more commands as a chain is that they are connected by a conjunction. Each command in a chain is recorded as an individual command (C), but the chain is indicated by drawing a single line above all the commands in the chain (e.g., $\overline{CCC}$).

EXAMPLES:

"Stand up and come over here." ($\overline{CC}$)
"Stand up, come here, and sit down." ($\overline{CCC}$)
"Wash your face, brush your teeth, and get ready for bed." ($\overline{CCC}$)
"Stop making so much noise and leave your sister alone." ($\overline{CC}$).

Command (C): Beta

The second class of commands is beta commands. As with alpha commands, these are scored as C in row 1. Beta commands are of two general types. One type includes scorable commands taking forms 1-6 above to which there is no opportunity for compliance. This occurs if: (1) the command is immediately followed (within 5 seconds) by parental verbiage that occurs prior to child compliance (this does not include chain commands, form 6 above; however, note that if there is a pause between the commands it is not scored as a chain command, but as a series of interrupted commands that are beta commands); (2) the parent complies to the command; or (3) the parent restricts the child's mobility precluding a compliance opportunity. The second type of beta command includes if/when . . . then conditional statements that offer the child a choice, and other vague commands.

    1. *If/when . . . then conditional statements that offer the child a choice.* These are automatically scored as beta commands.

EXAMPLES:

"If you sit down, then move the toys."
"Put it up there if you want to."
"When you finish, then put this on it."
"Don't spit on it if you hold it."
"If you want to, you can pick up the blocks."

2. *Vague commands.* Vague orders are those that do not specify the child behavior to be initiated or inhibited.

EXAMPLES:

"Be nice to your sister."
"Don't run away with yourself."
"Just be good for a while longer."
"Calm down."
"Act like a big boy, please."
"You think about that for a moment, young lady."
"You may do what you like."
"Be creative."
"Watch out."
"Do it right."
"Try your best."
"Think hard."
"See the army man."
"Just forget it."
"Be careful."

There are two exclusions to vague commands. Neither of these types of statements is scored.

a. *Commands referring to past or future behavior.*

EXAMPLES:

"If you'd picked it up last night, you'd have it done now."
"You may go outside after Ms. Brown leaves."
"You be nice to your father tonight."

b. *General statements and implied commands* in which reference to a specific behavior (motoric response) is omitted.

EXAMPLES:

"Time is up."
"Now it's my turn."

"Here's another block" (implying that the child is to do something with it).

"Time to go to bed."

"See!"

"Let's see."

The following are two general cues for recording commands (both alpha and beta).

1. *Time reference.* Commands must refer to ongoing behavior to be scorable. However, this rule is not tied entirely to verb tense. The critical factor is not verb tense, but the temporal contiguity of the parent's verbalizations with the behavior that is the referent; that is, if the parent is referring to behavior expected to be completed momentarily (future tense) or to behavior just completed, the event is close enough in time to be considered present. The "present" tense is best conceptualized by exclusion. Verbal statements referring to activities of yesterday, this morning (if the observation is in the afternoon), tonight, last Christmas, and so forth are not in the present. However, most references to activities that are occurring or can occur within the observational setting would be considered in the present tense. Notice the qualifier "most."

EXAMPLES:

"We will play dolls now." (C)

"You will have to pick up the toys next." (C)

"Are you going to hand me the truck?" (C)

2. *Initiation of behavior sequence.* A critical factor in differentiating certain commands from information is the child's mode of behavior preceding the parent's antecedent. The key point about the child's behavior is whether the child requested information (i.e., made a verbal request preceding the parent's statement) or did not request information (the parent gave a command following nonverbal behavior by the child).

EXAMPLES:

CHILD: (moves toward an object) (nonverbal)

PARENT: "No. No. No. Don't touch that!" (CCCC)

CHILD: "Can I turn on the tv?"
PARENT: "No, not now." (not scored; this is information that the child requested)

The one exception to the "initiation of behavior" issue is a statement of intention to perform an act made by the child. In this case the child is not requesting information.

EXAMPLE:

CHILD: "I'm going outside."
PARENT: "No, you aren't." (C)

Warning (W)

Any "if . . . then" statement in which the consequent event is aversive and is to be administered by either parent is considered a warning.

EXAMPLES:

"If you don't stop fussing, you'll have to go to your room."
"If you don't do as you're told, you'll have to sit in the corner."
"There will be no dessert for you tonight if you leave this room one more time."
"Your father will have to get mean with you if you don't shape up."

Question (Q)

Any interrogative to which the only appropriate child response is verbal is a question.
1. *General questions.*

EXAMPLES:

"What do you want to do?"
"Is that the roof?"
"Is there another one?"

"Where is the blue truck?"
"Are you ready?"
"Do you need some help?"
"Where are you going?"
"What color is it?"
"Why are the toys on the floor?"
"What is that?"
"Do you want a second helping?"
"Are you making a house?"
"Are you playing fireman?"
"Aren't you a horse now?"
"Do you see it?"
"What?"

2. *Tag questions.*

EXAMPLES:

"That's a block, isn't it?" (A,Q)
"You're a big boy, aren't you?" (R,Q)
"It will be OK, won't it?" (Q)

A statement consisting of a command plus tag question is scored solely as a question command (C).

EXAMPLE:

"Put up the blocks, will you?" (C)

3. *"Do you want . . ." questions.*

EXAMPLES:

"Do you want the coloring book?"
"Do you want to build a log cabin?"

4. *Questions by inflection.* Multiple-word statements with a rising inflection are scored as questions. Note that these same statements *without* the rising inflection might be scored as attends in other cases.

EXAMPLES:

CHILD: (playing with blocks)
PARENT: "*You are* playing with the blocks?" (Q)
PARENT: "*Playing* with the blocks?" (Q)
PARENT: "You're playing with the blocks." (A)

There are three exclusions to the general rules for scoring a question.

a. *Questions to which a nonverbal response is also appropriate.* These are scored as commands (C). This does not include questions beginning with "Do you want to . . . ?" which are always scored as questions.

EXAMPLE:
See section entitled "Command (C): Alpha," form 3, question commands.

b. *Single words.* Single words made into questions solely by inflection of the voice are information only and, therefore, not scorable. This does not include interrogatives such as who, what, when, where, how, or why.

EXAMPLES:

"Oh?"
"OK?"
"Really?"
"See?"
"Huh?"
"Yeah?"
"Going?"

c. *Questions reflecting the child's question.* As noted previously, the initiation of the interaction is important here. If the child initially asks a question (verbalization), the parent's reflection cannot be scored as a question. It is a nonscorable, or information, response. A reflection is terminated following the parent's initial reflective statement; that is, further reflections of the same question are scored as the appropriate parental behavior.

EXAMPLES:

CHILD: "When can I go outside, Mommy?"
PARENT: "When can you go out? Now, I guess." (not scorable)

CHILD: "When can I go outside, Mommy?"
PARENT: "When can you go out? You may go out now." (C)

CHILD: (playing quietly)
PARENT: "Do you want to go out? I want to clean up." (Q, followed by nonscorable information)

Attend (A)

Attends are descriptive phrases that follow and refer to the child's ongoing behavior or objects directly related to the child's activity, or the child's spatial orientation or appearance. Attends are usually neutral statements.

1. *Descriptions of activity.*

EXAMPLES:

"You've got a round block."
"You found me."
"You're pushing the car under the bridge."
"You're playing quietly."
"There goes the wagon."
"That's a long bridge."
"It's getting bigger."

The last three examples do not include a reference to the child. Therefore, it must be clear to the observer that the described object is directly related to the child's play.

2. *Descriptions of the child's spatial orientation or appearance.*

EXAMPLES:

"There you are."
"You're hiding behind the window."
"Oh, Johnny. You're all flushed."
"You're wearing the brown shirt today."

There are six exclusions to the general rules for scoring an attend.

a. *Reflection or repetition of the child's statement.* This is similar to the rule noted above for commands and questions concerning initiation of the interaction. If the child elicits the attend with a verbal statement or request for information, as opposed to a nonverbal cue, an attend is not scored.

EXAMPLES:

CHILD: "I've got the book now."
PARENT: "Oh, you've got it now." (not scorable)

CHILD: (picking up book)
PARENT: "Oh, you've got the book." (A)

CHILD: (registers a 15 on the cash register) "How much is that, Mommy?"
PARENT: "That's 15 dollars." (not scored)

CHILD: (registers a 15 on the cash register)
PARENT: "That's 15 dollars." (A)

b. *Child's name without reference to child's behavior.*

EXAMPLES:

"Johnny!" (not scorable)
"Here comes Johnny." (A)

c. *Descriptions of past or future behavior.* As discussed under commands above, the critical factor is not verb tense, but the time the behavioral referent is to occur.

EXAMPLES:

PARENT: "You always play with blocks at Grandma's." (not scorable)

PARENT: "Tonight you'll be watching tv." (not scorable)

CHILD: (stacking blocks)
PARENT: "You will have them all stacked up before long." (A)

d. *Inferences and interpretations.* Descriptions of the child's internal "state of being" (inferred) and interpretations about the child's activity constitute an exclusion to scoring an attend.

EXAMPLES:

"I think Johnny's all angry and upset."
"You really like that book."
"That seems so hard."

e. *Negative attends.* Descriptions or statements of what the child did not do are not scored as attends.

EXAMPLES:

"You're not building a house."
"You didn't let the bridge fall down."

f. *Criticisms or corrective statements.* Criticism of the child by any statement referring to the child's prior, ongoing, or future behavior that is negative in evaluation, states disapproval, or denotes less than average performance precludes an attending score.

EXAMPLES:

"That's not good at all."
"You've been a bad boy all morning."
"You're acting like a baby."
"You're so dumb you'll never get through the first grade."
"What a slow poke you are!"
"Wrong."
"No. That is a triangle."

There are two cues for recording an attend.

a. *Types of attends.* Attending is probably the most complex verbalization in the coding system. Two types of attending factor out in coding: (*a*) "You do . . . " and "You are . . . " statements; and (*b*) "X is . . . " or information-giving attends. The first type of attending remarks, the "You . . . " type, is easier to recognize, but less frequently used by parents than the second type (information attends).

EXAMPLES:

CHILD: (playing with dolls)
PARENT: "You sure do play with the dolls." (A; "You do . . . ")

CHILD: (standing in the corner)
PARENT: "You're over in the corner." (A; "You are . . . ")

CHILD: (getting dressed)
PARENT: "You've got on your blue jacket." (A; "You are . . . ")

CHILD: (coloring a picture of a tree)
PARENT: "That's a tree." (A; "X is . . . ")

CHILD: (building a log cabin)
PARENT: "There's the door of the cabin." (A; "X is . . . ")

b. *Attends must refer to the child's behavior.* It is not always apparent that an information-giving remark follows and refers to child behavior. The best available rule is that if an information statement ("X is . . . ") follows and refers to nonverbal child behavior, then an attend (A) is scored.

EXAMPLES:

CHILD: (playing with cash register)
PARENT: "That's a neat cash register." (A)

CHILD: (playing with cash register, pushing numbers)
PARENT: (points to key that opens drawer) "That opens the cash register." (not scorable; information was introduced that did not directly follow the child's play)

CHILD: (touching key that opens cash register)
PARENT: "That opens the cash register." (A)

Reward (R)

Any statement referring to the child or the child's prior, ongoing, or future behavior that is positive in evaluation or shows approval is a reward. Note that unlike commands, questions, and attends, temporal factors do not enter into the scoring of rewards. Physical affection is also scored as a reward.

1. *The positive behavior is specified (labeled verbal rewards).*

EXAMPLES:

"You made those two the best."
"Thank you for picking up the toys."
"Yeah, you built that super."
"What a nice job of cleaning up."
"You draw so well."
"That's a nicely colored picture."
"You're a good garage builder."
"That fort looks great, Joey."
"That will be a real good scrapbook."
"I like it when you do as you're told."

2. *The positive behavior is not specified (unlabeled verbal rewards).*

EXAMPLES:

"Thank you."
"Very nice."
"You're such a big boy."
"Good."
"Clever boy."
"Terrific."
"Wow!"
"Fantastic."
"Great."
"Wonderful."
"Right."
"Correct."
"All right!"
"There you go!"
"There you are."

The last two examples could be scored as attends, depending upon the context (e.g., if the child is crawling under a table, "There you go" would be an attend).

The following single words are considered information and, therefore, are not scored.

"Yeah."
"OK."
"Uh-huh."
"Oh."
"Yes."
"You're welcome."

3. *Descriptions of the child's behavior denoting better-than-average performance.*

EXAMPLES:

"You did that so fast."
"You're building it very high."
"You're so strong."
"How about you!"
"You put those away so fast."
"Tommy is doing so well."

To determine if statements of this type should be scored as rewards, cue on whether the statement implies that the child's performance is better than average. For example, "You're building it very slowly" might be scored as a R or not scored (excluded as a criticism), depending upon the context.

4. *Physical affection.*

EXAMPLES:

Hugging child
Kissing child
Ruffling child's hair
Clapping hands
Pulling child onto lap

Only each initiation of physical affection is credited as a reward (i.e., if the parent places and leaves an arm around the child or the child remains sitting in the parent's lap, the parent is scored for only one reward). Also, note that this category is physical *affection*. Grabbing the child by the arm and dragging the child across the room is not a reward. To be scored as a reward, physical contact must be initiated by the parent.

Child Responses (Category 2)

If the parent issues a command (C) or a warning (W), the observer must make a decision regarding the child's response and record that decision in row 2. There are three possible decisions: compliance (C), non-compliance (N), or no opportunity for compliance (leave row 2 blank).

An estimate of time must be made by the observer in order to assess the child's response. Upon termination of the parental command or warning, the observer should begin counting slowly from one to five. Tapping the foot may help. The three alternative child responses that constitute category 2 all depend on this rough estimate of the 5-second postcommand or postwarning interval.

Child Compliance (C)

Compliance is determined by the presence of an observable cue reflecting the *initiation* of compliance within 5 seconds of the termination of the parental command or warning. (Note that for a chain command, the observer begins counting at the termination of the final command in the chain.) There are four types of compliance.

1. Movement toward a specified goal object within 5 seconds
2. Initiation of a specified task within 5 seconds
3. Verbalization after a command for a verbal response within 5 seconds
4. Inhibition of a specified motor or verbal response for 5 seconds. Initiation of the inhibited response must also occur within 5 seconds of termination of the maternal command

EXAMPLES:

PARENT: "Come over here, please, Tommy." (C)
CHILD: (looks up and begins moving toward parent within 5 seconds) (C)

PARENT: "Hand me that pencil, please." (C)
CHILD: (pauses for 3 seconds, then hands pencil to parent) (C)

PARENT: "Tell me what color this block is." (C)
CHILD: (says a color within 5 seconds) (C)

PARENT: "Let me finish my sewing." (C)
CHILD: (colors in coloring book for 5 seconds) (C)

PARENT: "Stop coloring." (C)

CHILD: (continues coloring for 2 seconds, then stops for 5 seconds) (C)

PARENT: "She's tired. Leave her alone." (C)

CHILD: (3 seconds pass; picks up comic book and does not approach sister for 5 seconds) (C)

Child Noncompliance (N)

Noncompliance is determined by the presence of an observable cue reflecting (1) the failure to initiate compliance within 5 seconds of the termination of the parental command or warning; or (2) failure to maintain inhibition of a prohibited response for 5 seconds.

EXAMPLES:

PARENT: "Come here, Sam." (C)

CHILD: "Just a second." (continues playing for at least 5 seconds) (N)

PARENT: "Stop running." (C)

CHILD: (pauses briefly and then runs again after 2 seconds) (N)

PARENT: "Stop coloring." (C)

CHILD: (continues coloring for 6 seconds, then stops) (N)

As compliance/noncompliance to "stop" commands is particularly difficult to score, a further description of the scoring will be presented here. Like all alpha commands, "stop" commands are followed by a 5-second initiation period in which the child can *initiate* compliance to the command. If the child does not initiate compliance within this 5-second period, noncompliance is scored. The critical feature in scoring "stop" commands is that the child must also *maintain* compliance (inhibition of the response) for 5 seconds before compliance is scored. Thus, with "stop" commands the child must comply within the 5-second initiation period and then must maintain that compliance for a 5-second maintenance period. If the child does not maintain compliance for 5 seconds, noncompliance is scored. Thus the noncompliance (N) to "stop" commands may be scored in two ways: (1) if the child does not initiate compliance within 5 seconds or (2) if the child does not maintain compliance for 5 seconds.

EXAMPLES:

CHILD: (running)
PARENT: "Stop." (C)
CHILD: (stops running after 6 seconds) (N)

CHILD: (running)
PARENT: "Stop." (C)
CHILD: (stops running for 3 seconds, then begins to run again) (N)

"Stop" commands basically occur in three situations:

1. The child is engaged in a continuous ongoing behavior (running, rolling a car, etc.). The parent issues the "stop" command and the child must initiate compliance within 5 seconds and maintain compliance for 5 seconds (see above examples).
2. The child is not engaged in the inhibited behavior when the parent gives the "stop" command. For such commands of *prohibition*, the sole requirement for scoring compliance/noncompliance is that the child must maintain inhibition for 5 seconds. The 5-second initiation period is not scored, since the child has already initiated compliance by not being engaged in the behavior at the termination of the parental command.
3. A gray area in scoring "stop" commands occurs when the child is engaged in an intermittent behavior (e.g., throwing a block every second, hitting a drum every 2 seconds). When the parent gives a "stop" command, the observer begins to count the 5-second initiation period. When it is clear that the child has inhibited or changed the behavior, then the 5-second maintenance period is begun.

No-Opportunity-For-Compliance (leave row 2 blank)

1. *Vague commands.* This occurs when the command or warning is so broad or vague that the necessary observable cue defining compliance is unavailable. A special case is if/when . . . then conditional statements that offer the child a choice.

EXAMPLES:

CHILD: (approaches table lamp)

PARENT: "Be careful around that." (C)
CHILD: (picks up comic beside lamp) (not scorable)

CHILD: (playing with puzzle)
PARENT: "Think hard now." (C)
CHILD: (picks up piece) (not scorable)

CHILD: (standing)
PARENT: "If you sit down, then hand me the book." (C)
CHILD: (remains standing) (not scorable)

There is a gray area related to vague commands. For example, if the parent says, "Hurry up," score a command (C), but how does one decide if the child is actually hurrying? In some cases, it will be clear that the child is hurrying by an increase in motoric behavior. In other cases it is not so clear. Furthermore, if compliance can be scored, noncompliance ought to be able to be scored. How is the failure to hurry defined? If compliance is unclear, leave category 2 blank.

2. *Interrupted commands.* This occurs when the parent issues a scorable behavior (repeats the command, issues a new command, gives a warning, asks a question, or gives an attend or reward) or makes a nonscorable response before 5 seconds have elapsed since the initial command or warning and before the child initiates compliance to the initial command or warning. It is important to note that a verbalization can not interrupt unless it occurs following the sentence in which the command or warning occurs.

Following are three exclusions to the interrupted command in no-opportunity-for-compliance.

a. *Stop commands interrupted by positive consequences.* Compliance may be scored in row 2 if the parent rewards or attends to the child following a "stop" command, even if 5 seconds have not yet elapsed.

EXAMPLES:

CHILD: (running through house)
PARENT: "Stop that running!" (C)
CHILD: (2 seconds pass; stops running)
PARENT: (1 second passes) "That's a good boy for stopping." (R)

CHILD: (pulling dog's tail)
PARENT: "You'll hurt him. Don't pull." (C)

CHILD: (3 seconds pass; moves away from dog and starts playing with blocks) (C)

PARENT: (3 seconds pass) "Oh, you're playing with your blocks." (A)

b. *Chain commands.* Command components of a chain command are not scored as interruptions.

EXAMPLE:

PARENT: "Stand up and come over here." ($\overline{CC}$)

CHILD: (3 seconds pass; stands up) (C)

c. *Nonscorable one- or two-word phrases.* One- or two-word phrases (e.g., please, oh, OK, yes, the child's name, really, see, etc.) do not affect the scoring of child responses in category 2. The best cue for counting a nonscorable response as an interruption is the presence of a complete phrase. Any complete phrase that is not part of the sentence in which the command or warning occurs eliminates a potential score for category 2.

The following cues are used for recording/not recording child responses to interrupted and chain commands.

a. *Scoring/not scoring compliance to interrupted commands.* If the 5-second interval following a command is interrupted by any of the five scorable parental antecedents (command, warning, question, attend, or reward), the child response (row 2) in the column under the first command is left blank and the parental antecedent that interrupted the command is entered in row 1 of the next column. If a nonscorable parental response interrupts, row 2 is again left blank and the next scorable parental antecedent is entered in row 1 of the next column.

EXAMPLES:

CHILD: (playing with blocks)

PARENT: "Come here, please."

CHILD: (still playing after 2 seconds)

PARENT: "C'mon." (pause) "I want you to get over here."

CHILD: (looks, begins to approach parent)

SCORE: C C C
           C

CHILD: (screaming)
PARENT: "Stop that screaming this second!"
CHILD: (becomes quiet; 2 seconds pass)
PARENT: "Thank you. That's a good girl. Now come here."
CHILD: (continues to stand in one spot; 4 seconds pass)
PARENT: "You're so nice and quiet now."

SCORE: C R C R
          C
          R

The following commands are *not* interrupted:

"Put that over there and I'll do this."
"Don't pull his tail because you'll hurt him."
"Get me the block, will you?"
"Hand me the car." (2 seconds pass) "Johnny!"

b. *Scoring/not scoring compliance to chain commands.* If there is no pause between commands, the commands are scored as alpha commands (form 6, chain commands), and compliance is scored on the basis of initiation of compliance to the first command in the chain. In other words, in completing the child response (row 2) following a chain command, all commands except the first one are ignored.

EXAMPLE:

CHILD: (playing with blocks)
PARENT: "Pick those up and put them on the shelf."
CHILD: (still picking up blocks after 2 seconds)
PARENT: "Oh, and please wipe your nose."
CHILD: (still picking up blocks; 2 seconds pass without wiping nose)
PARENT: "Let's put this nice puzzle together, OK?"
CHILD: (pushes block box toward shelf; 5 seconds pass)
PARENT: "Well, what do you want to do?"
CHILD: (blows nose and smiles)

SCORE: $\overline{\text{CC}}$ C   C   Q
         C   N

3. *Physical interference with compliance.* This occurs when the parent complies with the command, physically guides the child to complete the required task, or physically restricts the child's mobility in any way.

Parental Consequences (Category 3)

A behavior can be scored in row 3 on only one condition: child compliance (C) has been scored in row 2. The best cue for category 3 is the one generated by the observers themselves. The following sequence should be used whenever (C) had been recorded in row 2: (1) count and/or tap foot slowly from one to five; (2) forget about the child; (3) watch the parent. The key to scoring rewards and attends in row 3 is that they occur within the 5-second interval, not that they directly refer to the child's act of compliance. The only parental behaviors that can be scored in row 3 are attends and rewards. All other scorable and nonscorable parental behaviors result in row 3 being left blank.

Reward (R)

The parent issues a reward (as defined under "Parental Antecedents") within 5 seconds after the initiation of compliance.

EXAMPLES:

PARENT: "Come here." (1 second passes)
CHILD: (begins approach; 2 seconds pass)
PARENT: "Thank you."

SCORE: C
        C
        R

PARENT: "Put that down."
CHILD: (4 seconds pass; sets vase down; 6 seconds pass)
PARENT: "That's a good boy for minding me."

SCORE: C R
        C

Attend (A)

The parent issues an attend (as defined under "Parental Antecedents") within 5 seconds after the initiation of compliance.

EXAMPLES:

PARENT: "Why don't you turn the page?"
CHILD: (3 seconds pass; turns page; 3 seconds pass)
PARENT: "Now you are looking at the picture."

SCORE: C
         C
         A

Failure-To-Reinforce-Compliance (leave row 3 blank)

1. *Failure to respond.* This occurs when the parent fails to respond with a reward or attend in the 5-second interval following the initiation of compliance.

2. *Interruption.* This occurs when the parent issues a command, question, warning, or nonscorable response within 5 seconds of the onset of compliance.

EXAMPLES:

PARENT: "Be quiet."
CHILD: (2 seconds pass; becomes quiet; 2 seconds pass)
PARENT: "What are you doing?"

SCORE: C   Q
         C

PARENT: "Would you stop that?"
CHILD: (4 seconds pass; quits banging fist on floor; 5 seconds pass)
PARENT: "Now find something to do."
CHILD: (remains on floor for 6 seconds)

SCORE: C   C
         C   N

Time-Out

Time-out is an action on the part of the parent that removes the child from positive reinforcement. There are two basic ways of scoring the initiation of TO, depending upon whether the parent implements TO correctly or incorrectly.

Correct Implementation

The parent issues a verbal statement to the child ("Since you didn't [states the command], you must sit in the chair until I say you can get up") and physically places the child in a chair in the corner within 5 seconds following child noncompliance.

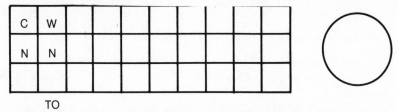

TO

In this example, a TO is placed below the column containing child noncompliance, signifying the correct implementation of TO.

Incorrect Implementation

The parent deviates from the standard TO procedure. This incorrect use of TO is noted in writing below the interval in which it occurs. Such deviations may include: TO initiated before the child has time (5 seconds) to respond to the parental command or warning; the late initiation of TO; failure to take the child to the TO chair; or failure to issue a verbal statement to the child when he or she is in the TO chair ("Since you didn't [state the command], you have to sit in the chair until I say you can get up").

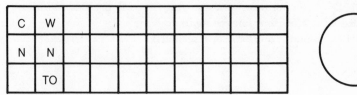

No Verbal
Statement

In this example, a TO is placed in the third row of the column containing child noncompliance signifying the incorrect implementation of TO, since the parent failed to issue a verbal statement to the child once he or she was seated in the TO chair.

Continue to record all scorable behavior and follow time intervals while the child is in TO.

The end of TO occurs when the parent permits the child to leave the chair. The end of TO is indicated by a slash (/) through the appropriate interval and column.

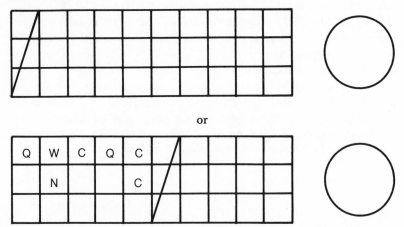

or

Child-initiated leaving the TO chair should be noted in writing below the interval in which it occurs.

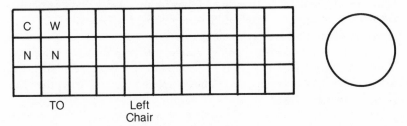

GENERAL SCORING RULES

1. To score a parental verbalization as a command (C), question (Q), or warning (W), a verb is a necessary but not a sufficient component.

EXAMPLES:

"How about some more wheels?" (not scored)
"Just a minute." (not scored)
"Just wait a minute." (C)

There is one exclusion to this rule: one word questions (how, what, etc.) are scored as Q.

2. Parental statements that reflect child verbiage (ordinarily scored as commands, questions, warnings, or attends) are not scored. A reflection is considered to be terminated following the parent's initial reflective statement; that is, further reflections of the same child verbiage are scored as the appropriate parental behavior. (See examples in appropriate sections of the manual.)

3. Only rewards (R) are not time-bound; in addition, it is the only parental behavior that can be scored when it reflects child verbiage.

4. If the parent commands the child to engage in a behavior that the child is already doing, then compliance is scored as long as the child is engaged in the activity at the termination of the parental command.

EXAMPLE:

CHILD: (stirring bowl of fudge)
PARENT: "Keep stirring." (C)
CHILD: (continues to stir for 2 seconds) (C)

However, if the child is already engaged in an activity and the parent refers to that activity by saying, "Are you doing [activity label]?" this is scored as a question, not as a command.

5. The key to scoring "going" statements is to focus on temporal cues; note "time reference" in the "Command (C): Beta" section. If the behavior is ongoing or expected to be completed momentarily, then the verbiage may be scored.

EXAMPLES:

"Are you going to color it red?" (C)
"You're going to put that on the table." (A or C, depending upon whether the parent is directing or following the child's activity)
"Are you going to set the table tonight?" (not scored — in the future)

6. Unfortunately, there is no general rule available for the many ways in which the word "see" is employed. The following are guidelines for scoring. (Note: "Look" is a clear-cut command, and there should be no scoring difficulties.)

a. Never scored
   (1) "See?"
   (2) "Let's see."
   (3) "See!"
b. Scored as a beta command (C)
   (1) "See the army man."
   (2) "See the clouds in the sky."
c. Scored as a command (C)
   (1) "See if you can find . . . "
   (2) "See if you can be quiet."
d. Scored as a question (Q)
   (1) "Do you see it?"
   (2) "Do you see what you have done?"

7. When the parent obviously stumbles or stutters over a sentence or phrase, the stumbling or stuttering is not considered scorable behavior.

EXAMPLES:

"Bill, try to . . . try to . . . try to pick them up." (C)
"Tell me . . . tell me . . . tell me how many blocks there are." (C)
"Tell me. Tell me right now!" (C, C)

SCORE SHEET

Child's Name _____
　　　　　　Last　　　　　First
Date _____ Time _____
Coder's Name _____
Session _____ Place _____

1

2

3

4

5

6

7

8

9

10

ROW 1	ROW 2	ROW 3	CIRCLE	OTHER
C command	C compliance	A attend	✓ inappropriate child beh.	TO time-out
W warning	N noncompliance	R reward	O appropriate child beh.	
Q question				
A attend				
R reward				

APPENDIX C.
PARENT HANDOUTS

There are two ways to decrease the frequency of your child's undesirable behavior: (1) increase his or her desirable behavior; or (2) decrease his or her undesirable behavior. The focus of Phase I is on increasing desirable behaviors.

What Phase I Skills Can Do

1. You can teach your child which behaviors you like, so that he or she can do them more often. Punishing bad behavior only gives your child information about what not to do.
2. You can learn to observe your child's behavior closely and to notice good things that he or she does. You will find your child has many desirable behaviors, not just undesirable ones.
3. These skills can help you to relax and have fun playing with your child. This will help to make time you spend playing with your child "quality" time.
4. As your child begins to enjoy being with you more, he or she will try harder to please you by doing the things you like.
5. You can be a model of good behavior for your child.
6. By increasing your child's desirable behaviors, you give him or her less time for undesirable ones.

What You Will Learn

1. You will learn to use your attention following desirable behavior. You will specifically learn two types of positive attention: (1) de-

scribing your child's behavior (attends), and (2) praising or rewarding.

2. You will learn to withhold your attention to your child (ignoring) after undesirable behavior. Note that ignoring can be used only when the behavior is not harmful or destructive. Harmful behaviors will be treated in Phase II.

3. You will learn consistent use of attention and ignoring.

PARENT HANDOUT 2: PRACTICING FOLLOWING AND ATTENDING (CHILD'S GAME)

Rules for Child's Game

1. *Child's activity.* Allow your child to choose the activity. Do not introduce anything new into his or her play. If your child changes activities, follow along, but do not change the activity yourself.

2. *Follow.* Watch with interest what your child is doing. A good way to describe this is "tailgating" your child.

3. *Attends.* Describe enthusiastically what he or she is doing (these are attends). Attends may be viewed as a play-by-play account or running commentary on your child's activity.

4. *Some participation and imitation.* Participate in your child's play by handing him or her materials or taking a turn. Be careful not to begin structuring the activity yourself. You also may participate by imitating his or her play. Remember that your child's activity is to be the center of your attention, so continue to describe his or her activity while working on your own.

5. *No questions or commands.* Do not ask any questions or give any commands. These interrupt and/or structure your child's play.

6. *No teaching.* Do not use this time to teach your child or to test his or her knowledge.

Homework

Play Child's Game with your child for one 10–15 minute period each day. (It may be helpful to schedule a time so you don't forget.) Make a record of each Child's Game on the Parent Record Sheet that follows.

This 10 to 15 minutes is for you to practice your attending skills. It also will be "quality" time for your child, since he or she will have your complete attention. Although Child's Game is a practice time, attending is a skill you can use throughout the day with your child.

PARENT RECORD SHEET (CHILD'S GAME)			
Date	Time Spent	Activity	Child's Response

Date	Time Spent	Activity	Child's Response

PARENT HANDOUT 3: REWARDS

There are three types of rewards.

1. Labeled verbal rewards include statements of exactly what your child did that you liked. This helps your child to know what is desirable behavior and, therefore, they should be used more often than unlabeled verbal rewards (e.g., "Good boy for picking up the blocks").
2. Unlabeled verbal rewards do not tell your child exactly which behavior is being rewarded (e.g., "That's great!").
3. Physical rewards are hugs, kisses, pats, and so forth.

Rewards are not supposed to replace attends. Rather, they are to be used together. Remember that they are both types of positive attention.

Rewards and attends should be used following desirable behavior to help increase those behaviors.

Homework

Continue to play Child's Game with your child for one 10- to 15-minute period each day. Record each Child's Game on your Parent Record Sheet. Practice using both rewards and attends. Remember: the child chooses the activity; you are to reward, attend, and follow desirable behavior; there should be some imitation and participation on your part; no questions, commands, or teaching should take place.

PARENT HANDOUT 4: EXAMPLES OF REWARDS

Some Verbal Rewards

1. "I like it when you . . . "
2. "That's a beautiful . . . " (whatever the child makes)
3. "Good boy for . . . " (picking up the blocks, doing what I asked, etc.)
4. "Hey, you're really sharp, you . . . "
5. "That's great, it really looks like . . . "
6. "Wow!"
7. "That's really good, I wish I could do that."

8. "You're doing just what Mommy wants you to do."
9. "My! Your minding Daddy so well."
10. "My! That . . . (road, tower) was so nice."
11. "You do a good job at . . . "
12. "That's very nice [or good]." (pointing)
13. "You're such a big girl for . . . "
14. "Mommy's very proud of you for . . . "
15. "See what nice things you do."
16. "Those . . . (pictures, towers) are real pretty."
17. "I like playing this with you."
18. "This is such fun."
19. One word "quickies": "Beautiful!" "Fine!" "Great!" Gorgeous!" "Tremendous!"

Some Physical Rewards

1. Pat arm, shoulder.
2. Hug.
3. Rub head.
4. Squeeze arm or waist.
5. Pat his or her bottom.
6. Give a kiss.

Rewards should always be paired with telling a child *exactly what she or he did/is doing that pleases you.*

PARENT HANDOUT 5: IGNORING

This is a major way to decrease your child's inappropriate behavior. However, it is very important that you use ignoring *every* time a particular behavior occurs; otherwise, the behavior will become worse instead of better.

There are three things you should do when you ignore your child's behavior.

1. No eye contact or nonverbal cues: turn your back (or at least turn 90° from your child) so that he or she cannot get attention (like a frown or a glance) from you.
2. No verbal contact: once you have started ignoring, do not say anything to your child. If you do, you are no longer ignoring him

or her; instead, you are rewarding your child for behaving inappropriately.

3. No physical contact: you may have to stand up or even leave the room to avoid giving physical attention to your child.

As soon as the bad behavior begins, start ignoring. Note: There are some behaviors you should not ignore. For example, whenever there is a chance of damage to the child, someone else, or to property, a punishment procedure is appropriate.

As soon as the inappropriate behavior has stopped, stop ignoring. At this time reward or attend to your child's appropriate behavior.

PARENT HANDOUT 6: PHASE II

As noted in Parent Handout 1, there are two ways to decrease the frequency of your child's undesirable behavior: (1) increase his or her desirable behavior, using the skills you learned in Phase I; (2) decrease his or her undesirable behavior, using the skills you now will learn in Phase II.

Phase II skills are used in two ways:

1. To get your child to do the things that you ask him or her to do
2. To get your child to stop doing the things you find undesirable

There will not be any specific practice times at home for these skills, as there were for Phase I skills. After you have mastered Phase II skills in the clinic, they are employed in the home.

Phase II skills do *not* replace the skills you have already mastered. Be sure to continue to praise and attend to your child's desirable behavior. Also continue to ignore minor problem behaviors. Be consistent with the behaviors you decide to ignore. (It may be useful to review Parent Handouts 1–5). Phase II skills are effective *only* when used in combination with Phase I skills.

PARENT HANDOUT 7: PHASE II PRACTICE (PARENT'S GAME)

What Is Parent's Game?

Parent's Game is simply a practice time for learning new skills to use with your child. The situations in Parent's Game may not be exactly like those you encounter at home, but you can master the skills to be used in those situations at home in this practice time.

In Parent's Game, unlike Child's Game, you are to structure the activity and have your child do what you ask. In other words, you are to be in control.

Rules for Parent's Game

1. *Clear concise commands.* When you want your child to do something, use a simple, direct command. This way you can be sure that your child understands exactly what you expect. Give only *one* command at a time. Give only commands that you are willing to take the time to enforce. If you are going to provide a rationale, give it *before* the command.

2. *No questions.* Do not use a question when you want your child to do something (e.g., "Would you clean up your room now?"). When you ask your child a question, you give him or her a choice and you must be willing to accept no as an answer.

3. *Praise compliance.* After you give a command, stop and wait for your child's response. If he or she does what you want, immediately praise or attend to him or her. Compliance is desirable behavior. As you learned in Phase I, you can increase this behavior by using your attention contingent on its occurrence.

4. *Warning.* If your child does not comply with your command after a reasonable amount of time (probably about 5 seconds), give him or her a warning. Do *not* repeat your command. This will help stop you from becoming angry as you repeatedly ask your child to do something.

Warnings are "if . . . then" statements (e.g., "If you don't pick up that block, you will have to sit in the chair!"). Warnings should be given in a stern, firm voice so that your child knows that you are serious.

5. *Praise compliance.* Again, if your child complies following a warning, immediately praise or attend to him or her.

6. *Time-out (TO).*

   a. If your child does not start to comply to a warning within 5 seconds, you must use TO. The form of TO that is usually best is putting your child in a chair facing a corner. Take your child firmly by the hand and place him or her on the chair. Say, "Since you didn't _____, you have to sit in the chair until I say you can get up."

   Use gestures and motions that show your displeasure. Do not discuss or reason with your child while taking him or her to TO or while he or she is in TO. Completely ignore his or her temper tantrums, shouting, protesting, or promises to behave.

b. The first time your child gets off the chair without your permission, immediately and firmly place him or her back on the chair and say, "If you get off that chair again, I'm going to spank you." Your child gets this warning *once*.

c. If your child gets off the chair again (either after this warning or in subsequent uses of TO), administer two (and only two) spanks on the bottom with your hand (do *not* use any other object). Then place your child firmly back in TO and say, "If you get off the chair again, I'll spank you again."

d. The child should be in TO for about 3 minutes. The most important rule is that release from TO must be contingent upon sitting quietly in the chair for 15 seconds.

e. After your child has been quiet for an appropriate length of time, go to him or her and remove the child from TO.

f. Return to the activity that resulted in TO and repeat the command with which he or she originally refused to comply. Then follow the rules listed above.

7. To summarize, the sequence is as follows:

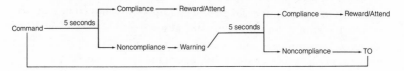

Remember, never give your child a command unless you are prepared to follow the above procedure. If you really don't think it's important, don't make it a command. The Parent Record Sheet to be used follows.

PARENT RECORD SHEET (PHASE II)

					Time-Out	
					---	---
Date	Time	Command/ Warning	Child's Response	Reward/Attend for Compliance	Duration	Number of Spanks

APPENDIX D.
SOCIAL LEARNING
CRITERION TESTS
AND SCORING KEYS

SOCIAL LEARNING CRITERION, RATIONALE

Name _____

Date _____

Fill in the blanks in the following statements. In some cases there are several correct responses possible.

1. Behavior can be ch _____.
2. The social learning approach assumes that you are responsible for your own _____.

Circle the best answer.

3. A critical factor for achieving success in this program is
   a. authority
   b. insight
   c. consistency
   d. all of the above
4. Which of the following is a negative effect of punishment?
   a. It may be emotionally upsetting for you and your child.
   b. It has no effect on compliance per se.

c. Your child may avoid you.

d. All of the above are true.

Circle **T** if the statement is true; circle **F** if the statement is false.

5. Often when children behave in disturbing ways, their parents have unknowingly taught them to do so. **T F**

6. A social learning approach to child behavior is designed primarily to teach children to be popular. **T F**

7. A problem child acts the way he or she does because he or she was born that way. **T F**

8. You can teach your child both positive and problem behaviors. **T F**

9. Punishment will permanently eliminate a problem behavior. **T F**

SOCIAL LEARNING CRITERION, PHASE I

Name _____

Date _____

Fill in the blanks in the following statements. In some cases there are several correct responses available.

1. Follow behaviors you wish to _____ with reinforcing events.

2. Behaviors can be weakened by no longer _____ them.

3. A delay in reinforcement can be bridged by t_____ your child what you are praising him or her for.

4. When teaching something new, _____ each new behavior right away.

5. It is possible to accidentally train your child to engage in inappropriate ("bad") behavior by occasionally "giving in" and _____ _____ to the bad behavior.

6. A major assumption is that a child will work for adults' _____, which may be positive or negative.

7. To change an undesirable behavior, parents must be very _____ in not rewarding that behavior.

8. To get a new behavior going, reinforce it _____ _____ it occurs.

9. To keep the behavior going, reward _____.

10. Reinforcing small steps on the way to the desired behavior is called s_____.

11-12. The task in teaching new behavior is to find ways to _____ the undesirable behavior and to strengthen the _____ behaviors, and to pair these two events to that the child learns what is expected of him or her more quickly.

13. The parent who tries to teach children mainly by scolding instead of praising may be caught in the _____ trap.

14-15. To get out of the criticism trap, you need to _____ more and _____ less.

16. The person in the family who gives the most punishment receives the most _____.

17-18. Two general types of reinforcers are _____ reinforcers, such as "Thank you" or a smile and _____ reinforcers, such as money or candy.

Circle **T** if the statement is true; circle **F** if the statement is false.

19. If the reward is a large one, you only need to reward the child once to get his or her behavior to change. **T F**

20. You can cause your child's good behavior to occur less often or even to disappear by ignoring it. **T F**

21. An advantage of social reinforcers over material reinforcers is that they are more realistic in terms of what the child can expect to find as an adult in the real world as reinforcement for his or her behavior. **T F**

SOCIAL LEARNING CRITERION, PHASE II

Name _____

Date _____

Fill in the blanks in the following statements. In some cases there are several correct responses possible.

1. An event that occurs following behavior and weakens the future rate of such behavior is called a _____.

2. Most of the rules about reinforcers apply to punishment, except that we are talking about _____ rather than strengthening behavior.

3-4. In itself, use of punishment is not immoral or moral. Punishment should be used when the long-term effects from the use of punishment lead to more _____ than harm. Punishment should not be used when the long-term effects are more _____ than good.

5. Punishment is one way of _____ behavior.

6. When you do use punishment, it should be given _____ after the bad behavior.

7-8. Punishment involves presenting _____ consequences or _____ reinforcing consequences.

9. If a behavior you desire your child to engage in is relatively complex, break your commands into the _____ steps necessary to achieve that behavior.

10. When your child complies to a command, it is best to reinforce him or her frequently and _____. Your reinforcement should come as soon as he or she initiates the behavior.

11. Time-out means to remove your child from all sources of _____ _____.

12. When using ignoring or time-out to weaken a behavior, remember to use _____ to strengthen the positive behaviors, and to pair these two events so that the child learns what is expected of him or her more quickly.

13. If you depend upon punishment alone to train your child,

you will become (more/less) powerful as a reinforcing agent to your child.

14-15. To be effective, punishment must prevent avoidance and _____ from the punisher, and minimize _____ reactions.

16. To be effective, the punisher should not provide a _____ of aggressive behavior.

17. Effective punishment makes use of a _____ signal, usually in the form of words.

18. Good punishment is carried out in a _____, matter-of-fact way.

19. If you really want a behavior to stop, you should not punish it sometimes and _____ it other times.

20. You may have to use punishment if the problem behavior causes your child to _____ himself or herself or others.

KEY: SOCIAL LEARNING CRITERION, RATIONALE

1. changed
2. behavior
3. c.
4. d.
5. T
6. F
7. F
8. T
9. F

KEY: SOCIAL LEARNING CRITERION, PHASE I

1. strengthen
2. reinforcing
3. telling
4. reinforce
5. paying attention
6. attention
7. consistent

8. every time
9. once in a while, intermittently, occasionally
10. shaping
11. weaken
12. desirable
13. criticism
14. praise
15. criticize
16. punishment
17. social
18. material
19. F
20. T
21. T

KEY: SOCIAL LEARNING CRITERION, PHASE II

1. punishment, punisher
2. weakening
3. good
4. harmful
5. weakening
6. immediately
7. negative, aversive
8. taking away
9. small, short
10. immediately
11. positive reinforcement
12. reinforcement
13. less
14. escape
15. fearful, emotional
16. model
17. warning
18. calm
19. reinforce
20. hurt

REFERENCES

Adkins, D. A., & Johnson, S. M. *What behaviors may be called deviant for children? A comparison of two approaches to behavior classification.* Paper presented at the Western Psychological Association Convention, Portland, Oregon, April 1972.

Alexander, J. F., Barton, C., Schiavo, S. R., & Parsons, B. V. Systems-behavioral intervention with families of delinquents: Therapist characteristics, family behavior, and outcome. *Journal of Consulting and Clinical Psychology,* 1976, *44,* 656–664.

Ames, L. B. *Child care and development.* Philadelphia: Lippincott, 1970.

Atkeson, B. M., & Forehand, R. Parent behavioral training for problem children: An examination of studies using multiple outcome measures. *Journal of Abnormal Child Psychology,* 1978, *6,* 449–460.

Atkeson, B. M., & Forehand, R. Conduct disorders. In E. J. Mash & L. G. Terdal (Eds.), *Behavioral assessment of childhood disorders.* New York: Guilford Press, 1981.

Azrin, N. H., & Foxx, R. M. *Toilet training in less than a day.* New York: Simon & Schuster, 1974.

Azrin, N. H., Hontos, P. T., & Besalel-Azrin, V. Elimination of enuresis without a conditioning apparatus: An extension by office instruction of the child and parents. *Behavior Therapy,* 1979, *10,* 14–19.

Azrin, N. H., Sneed, T. J., & Foxx, R. M. Dry-bed training: Rapid elimination of childhood enuresis. *Behaviour Research and Therapy,* 1974, *12,* 147–156.

Barkley, R. A. *Hyperactive children: A handbook for diagnosis and treatment.* New York: Guilford Press, 1981.

Barton, E. S., Guess, D., Garcia, E., & Baer, D. M. Improvement of retardates' mealtime behaviors by timeout procedures using multiple baseline techniques. *Journal of Applied Behavior Analysis,* 1970, *3,* 77–84.

Baum, C., & Forehand, R. Long term follow-up assessment of parent training by use of multiple outcome measures. *Behavior Therapy,* in press.

Beck, A. T. *Depression: Causes and treatment.* Philadelphia: University of Pennsylvania Press, 1967.

Beck, A. T., Rush, A. J., Shaw, B. F., & Emery, G. *Cognitive therapy of depression.* New York: Guilford Press, 1979.

Becker, W. C. The relationship of factors in parental ratings of self and each other to the behavior of kindergarten children as rated by mothers, fathers, and teachers. *Journal of Consulting Psychology*, 1960, *24*, 507–527.

Becker, W. C. *Parents are teachers: A child management program.* Champaign, Ill.: Research Press, 1971.

Becker, W. C. *Review tests for Parents Are Teachers.* Champaign, Ill.: Research Press, 1975.

Berkowitz, B. P., & Graziano, A. M. Training parents as behavior therapists: A review. *Behaviour Research and Therapy*, 1972, *10*, 297–317.

Bernal, M. E., Klinnert, M. D., & Schultz, L. A. Outcome evaluation of behavioral parent training and client-centered parent counseling for children with conduct problems. *Journal of Applied Behavior Analysis*, 1980, *13*, 677–691.

Bernhardt, A. J., & Forehand, R. The effects of labeled and unlabeled praise upon lower and middle class children. *Journal of Experimental Child Psychology*, 1975, *19*, 536–543.

Breckenridge, M. E., & Vincent, E. L. *Child development: Physical growth through adolescence* (5th ed.). Philadelphia: Saunders, 1965.

Breiner, J. L., & Forehand, R. An assessment of the effects of parent training on clinic-referred children's school behavior. *Behavioral Assessment*, 1981, *3*, 31–42.

Caplan, G. *Principles of preventive psychiatry.* New York: Basic Books, 1964.

Christophersen, E. R., Barnard, J. D., Ford, D., & Wolf, M. M. The family training program: Improving parent–child interaction patterns. In E. J. Mash, L. C. Handy, & L. A. Hamerlynck (Eds.), *Behavior modification approaches to parenting.* New York: Brunner/Mazel, 1976.

Ciminero, A. R., Calhoun, K. S., & Adams, H. E. *Handbook of behavioral assessment.* New York: Wiley, 1977.

Ciminero, A. R., & Drabman, R. S. Current developments in the behavioral assessment of children. In B. B. Lahey & A. E. Kazdin (Eds.), *Advances in clinical child psychology* (Vol. 1). New York: Plenum, 1977.

Conger, R. D. The assessment of dysfunctional family systems. In B. B. Lahey & A. E. Kazdin (Eds.), *Advances in clinical child psychology* (Vol. 4). New York: Plenum, in press.

Conway, J. G., & Bucher, B. D. Transfer and maintenance of behavior change in children: A review and suggestions. In E. J. Mash, L. A. Hamerlynck, & L. C. Handy (Eds.), *Behavior modification and families.* New York: Brunner/Mazel, 1976.

Cowen, E. L., Huser, J., Beach, D. R., & Rappaport, J. Parental perceptions of young children and their relation to indexes of adjustment. *Journal of Consulting and Clinical Psychology*, 1970, *34*, 97–103.

Doleys, D. M. Assessment and treatment of childhood encopresis. In A. J. Finch, Jr., & P. C. Kendall (Eds.), *Clinical treatment and research in child psychopathology.* New York: Spectrum, 1979. (a)

Doleys, D. M. Assessment and treatment of childhood enuresis. In A. J. Finch, Jr., & P. C. Kendall (Eds.), *Clinical treatment and research in child psychopathology.* New York: Spectrum, 1979. (b)

Dreikurs, R. *Children: The challenge.* New York: Hawthorn Books, 1964.

Dreyer, C. A., & Dreyer, A. S. Family dinner time as a unique behavior habitat.

Family Process, 1973, *12,* 291–301.

Evans, I. M., & Nelson, R. O. Assessment of child behavior problems. In A. R. Ciminero, K. S. Calhoun, & H. E. Adams (Eds.), *Handbook of behavioral assessment.* New York: Wiley, 1977.

Flanagan, S., Adams, H. E., & Forehand, R. A comparison of four instructional techniques for teaching parents the use of time-out. *Behavior Therapy,* 1979, *10,* 94–102.

Fleischman, M. J. Using parenting salaries to control attrition and cooperation in therapy. *Behavior Therapy,* 1979, *10,* 111–116.

Fleischman, M. J., Shilton, P. E., & Arthur, J. L. *Client Readiness Scale.* Paper presented at the Pre-AABT Family Conference, San Francisco, December 1979.

Forehand, R. Child noncompliance to parental requests: Behavioral analysis and treatment. In M. Hersen, R. M. Eisler, & P. M. Miller (Eds.), *Progress in behavior modification* (Vol. 5). New York: Academic Press, 1977.

Forehand, R., & Atkeson, B. M. Generality of treatment effects with parents as therapists: A review of assessment and implementation procedures. *Behavior Therapy,* 1977, *8,* 575–593.

Forehand, R., Cheney, T., & Yoder, P. Parent behavior training: Effects on the non-compliance of a deaf child. *Journal of Behavior Therapy and Experimental Psychiatry,* 1974, *5,* 281–283.

Forehand, R., Griest, D., & Wells, K. C. Parent behavioral training: An analysis of the relationship among multiple outcome measures. *Journal of Abnormal Child Psychology,* 1979, *7,* 229–242.

Forehand, R., & King. H. E. Pre-school children's non-compliance: Effects of short-term therapy. *Journal of Community Psychology,* 1974, *2,* 42–44.

Forehand, R., & King, H. E. Noncompliant children: Effects of parent training on behavior and attitude change. *Behavior Modification,* 1977, *1,* 93–108.

Forehand, R., King, H. E., Peed, S., & Yoder, P. Mother–child interactions: Comparisons of a non-compliant clinic group and a non-clinic group. *Behaviour Research and Therapy,* 1975, *13,* 79–84.

Forehand, R., & MacDonough, T. S. Response contingent time-out: An examination of outcome data. *European Journal of Behavioural Analysis and Modification,* 1975, *1,* 109–115.

Forehand, R., & Peed, S. Training parents to modify noncompliant behavior of their children. In A. J. Finch, Jr., & P. C. Kendall (Eds.), *Treatment and research in child psychopathology.* New York: Spectrum, 1979.

Forehand, R., Peed, S., Roberts, M., McMahon, R. J., Griest, D. L., & Humphreys, L. *Coding manual for scoring mother–child interaction* (3rd ed.). Unpublished manuscript, University of Georgia, 1978.

Forehand, R., & Scarboro, M. E. An analysis of children's oppositional behavior. *Journal of Abnormal Child Psychology,* 1975, *3,* 27–31.

Forehand, R., Sturgis, E. T., McMahon, R. J., Aguar, D., Green, K., Wells, K., & Breiner, J. Parent behavioral training to modify child noncompliance: Treatment generalization across time and from home to school. *Behavior Modification,* 1979, *3,* 3–25.

Forehand, R., Wells, K. C., & Griest, D. L. An examination of the social validity of a parent training program. *Behavior Therapy,* 1980, *11,* 488–502.

Forehand, R., Wells, K. C., & Sturgis, E. T. Predictors of child noncompliant behavior in the home. *Journal of Consulting and Clinical Psychology*, 1978, *46*, 179.

Gardner, H. L., Forehand, R., & Roberts, M. Time-out with children: Effects of an explanation and brief parent training on child and parent behaviors. *Journal of Abnormal Child Psychology*, 1976, *4*, 277-288.

Gersten, J. C., Langner, T. S., Eisenberg, J. G., Simcha-Fagen, O., & McCarthy, E. D. Stability and change in types of behavioral disturbance of children and adolescents. *Journal of Abnormal Child Psychology*, 1976, *4*, 111-127.

Glogower, F., & Sloop, E. W. Two strategies of group training of parents as effective behavior modifiers. *Behavior Therapy*, 1976, *7*, 177-184.

Graziano, A. M. Parents as behavior therapists. In M. Hersen, R. M. Eisler, & P. M. Miller (Eds.), *Progress in behavior modification* (Vol. 4). New York: Academic Press, 1977.

Griest, D. L., Forehand, R., & Wells, K. C. Follow-up assessment of parent behavioral training: An analysis of who will participate. *Child Study Journal*, in press.

Griest, D. L., Forehand, R., Wells, K. C., & McMahon, R. J. An examination of differences between nonclinic and behavior problem clinic-referred children and their mothers. *Journal of Abnormal Psychology*, 1980, *89*, 497-500.

Griest, D., Wells, K. C., & Forehand, R. An examination of predictors of maternal perceptions of maladjustment in clinic-referred children. *Journal of Abnormal Psychology*, 1979, *88*, 277-281.

Hanf, C., & Kling, J. *Facilitating parent–child interaction: A two-stage training model*. Unpublished manuscript, University of Oregon Medical School, 1973.

Haynes, S. N. *Principles of behavioral assessment*. New York: Gardner Press, 1978.

Hersen, M., & Barlow, D. H. *Single-case experimental designs*. New York: Pergamon Press, 1976.

Hetherington, E. M., Cox, M., & Cox, R. Play and social interaction in children following divorce. *Journal of Social Issues*, 1979, *5*, 26-49.

Hobbs, S. A., & Forehand, R. Differential effects of contingent and noncontingent release from time-out on noncompliance and disruptive behavior of children. *Journal of Behavior Therapy and Experimental Psychiatry*, 1975, *6*, 256-257.

Hobbs, S. A., Forehand, R., & Murray, R. G. Effects of various durations of time-out on the non-compliant behavior of children. *Behavior Therapy*, 1978, *9*, 652-656.

Hughes, H. M., & Haynes, S. N. Structured laboratory observation in the behavioral assessment of parent–child interactions: A methodological critique. *Behavior Therapy*, 1978, *9*, 428-447.

Humphreys, L., Forehand, R., McMahon, R., & Roberts, M. Parent behavioral training to modify child noncompliance: Effects on untreated siblings. *Journal of Behavior Therapy and Experimental Psychiatry*, 1978, *9*, 235-238.

Johansson, S. *Compliance and noncompliance in young children*. Unpublished doctoral dissertation, University of Oregon, 1971.

Johnson, S. M., Bolstad, O. D., & Lobitz, G. K. Generalization and contrast phenomena in behavior modification with children. In E. J. Mash, L. A. Hamerlynck, & L. C. Handy (Eds.), *Behavior modification and families.* New York: Brunner/Mazel, 1976.

Johnson, S. M., & Eyberg, S. Evaluating outcome data: A reply to Gordon. *Journal of Consulting and Clinical Psychology,* 1975, *43,* 917-919.

Johnson, S. M., & Lobitz, G. K. The personal and marital adjustment of parents as related to observed child deviance and parenting behaviors. *Journal of Abnormal Child Psychology,* 1974, *2,* 193-207. (a)

Johnson, S. M., & Lobitz, G. K. Parental manipulation of child behavior in home observations. *Journal of Applied Behavior Analysis,* 1974, *7,* 23-31. (b)

Johnson, S. M., Wahl, G., Martin, S., & Johansson, S. How deviant is the normal child? A behavioral analysis of the preschool child and his family. In R. D. Rubin, J. P. Brady, & J. D. Henderson (Eds.), *Advances in behavior therapy* (Vol. 4). New York: Academic Press, 1973.

Kazdin, A. E. Assessing the clinical or applied importance of behavior change through social validation. *Behavior Modification,* 1977, *1,* 427-452.

Kazdin, A. E. *Research design in clinical psychology.* New York: Harper & Row, 1980.

Kent, R. N., & Foster, S. L. Direct observational procedures: Methodological issues in naturalistic settings. In A. R. Ciminero, K. S. Calhoun, & H. E. Adams (Eds.), *Handbook of behavioral assessment.* New York: Wiley, 1977.

Kimmel, D., & van der Veen, F. Factors of marital adjustment in Locke's Marital Adjustment Test. *Journal of Marriage and the Family,* 1974, *36,* 57-63.

Kovacs, M., & Beck, A. T. Maladaptive cognitive structure in depression. *American Journal of Psychiatry,* 1978, *135,* 525-533.

Krumboltz, J. D., & Krumboltz, H. B. *Changing children's behavior.* Englewood Cliffs, N.J.: Prentice-Hall, 1972.

LaBarbera, J. D., & Lewis, S. Fathers who undermine children's treatment: A challenge for the clinician. *Journal of Clinical Child Psychology,* 1980, *9,* 204-206.

Landauer, T. K., Carlsmith, J. M., & Lepper, M. Experimental analysis of the factors determining obedience of four-year-old children to adult females. *Child Development,* 1970, *41,* 601-611.

Lipinski, D., & Nelson, R. Problems in the use of naturalistic observation as a means of behavioral assessment. *Behavior Therapy,* 1974, *5,* 341-351.

Lobitz, G. K., & Johnson, S. M. Normal versus deviant children: A multi-method comparison. *Journal of Abnormal Child Psychology,* 1975, *3,* 353-374.

Locke, H. J., & Wallace, K. M. Short marital adjustment and prediction tests: Their reliability and validity. *Marriage and Family Living,* 1959, *21,* 251-255.

MacDonough, T., & Forehand, R. Response-contingent time out: Important parameters in behavior modification with children. *Journal of Behavior Therapy and Experimental Psychiatry,* 1973, *4,* 231-236.

Marholin, D., Siegel, L. J., & Phillips, D. Treatment and transfer: A search for empirical procedures. In M. Hersen, R. M. Eisler, & P. M. Miller (Eds.),

Progress in behavior modification (Vol. 3). New York: Academic Press, 1976.

Martin, B. Brief family intervention: Effectiveness and the importance of including the father. *Journal of Consulting and Clinical Psychology,* 1977, *45,* 1002-1010.

Martin, S., Johnson, S. M., Johansson, S., & Wahl, G. The comparability of behavioral data in laboratory and natural settings. In E. J. Mash, L. A. Hamerlynck, & L. C. Handy (Eds.), *Behavior modification and families.* New York: Brunner/Mazel, 1976.

Mash, E. J., & Terdal, L. G. (Eds.). *Behavioral assessment of childhood disorders.* New York: Guilford Press, 1981.

McMahon, R. J., & Davies, G. R. A behavioral parent training program and its side effects on classroom behavior. *B. C. Journal of Special Education,* 1980, *4,* 165-174.

McMahon, R. J., & Forehand, R. Nonprescription behavior therapy: Effectiveness of a brochure in teaching mothers to correct their children's inappropriate mealtime behavior. *Behavior Therapy,* 1978, *9,* 814-820.

McMahon, R. J., & Forehand, R. Self-help behavior therapies in parent training. In B. B. Lahey & A. E. Kazdin (Eds.), *Advances in clinical child psychology* (Vol. 3). New York: Plenum, 1980.

McMahon, R. J., & Forehand, R. Suggestions for evaluating self-administered materials in parent training. *Child Behavior Therapy,* 1981, *3,* 38-39.

McMahon, R. J., Forehand, R., & Griest, D. L. Effects of knowledge of social learning principles on enhancing treatment outcome and generalization in a parent training program. *Journal of Consulting and Clinical Psychology,* 1981, *49,* 526-532.

McMahon, R. J., Forehand, R., Griest, D. L., & Wells, K. C. Who drops out of treatment during parent behavioral training? *Behavioral Counseling Quarterly,* 1981, *1,* 79-85.

Metcalfe, M., & Goldman, E. Validation of an inventory for measuring depression. *British Journal of Psychiatry,* 1965, *111,* 240-242.

Miller, W. H. *Systematic parent training: Procedures, cases, and issues.* Champaign, Ill.: Research Press, 1975.

Nay, W. R. A systematic comparison of instructional techniques for parents. *Behavior Therapy,* 1975, *6,* 14-21.

Nay, W. R. Parents as real-life reinforcers: The enhancement of parent training effects across conditions other than training. In A. P. Goldstein & F. H. Kanfer (Eds.), *Maximizing treatment gains: Transfer enhancement in psychotherapy.* New York: Academic Press, 1979.

O'Brien, F., & Azrin, N. H. Developing proper mealtime behaviors of the institutionalized retarded. *Journal of Applied Behavior Analysis,* 1972, *5,* 389-399.

O'Dell, S. Training parents in behavior modification: A review. *Psychological Bulletin,* 1974, *81,* 418-433.

O'Dell, S. L., Flynn, J. M., & Benlolo, L. A. A comparison of parent training techniques in child behavior modification. *Journal of Behavior Therapy and Experimental Psychiatry,* 1977, *8,* 261-268.

O'Dell, S. L., Tarler-Benlolo, L. A., & Flynn, J. M. An instrument to measure knowledge of behavioral principles as applied to children. *Journal of Behavior Therapy and Experimental Psychiatry*, 1979, *10*, 29-34.

Oltmanns, T. F., Broderick, J. E., & O'Leary, K. D. Marital adjustment and the efficacy of behavior therapy with children. *Journal of Consulting and Clinical Psychology*, 1977, *45*, 724-729.

Patterson, G. R. Interventions for boys with conduct problems: Multiple settings, treatments, and criteria. *Journal of Consulting and Clinical Psychology*, 1974, *42*, 471-481.

Patterson, G. R. *Families: Applications of social learning to family life* (Rev. ed). Champaign, Ill.: Research Press, 1975.

Patterson, G. R. The aggressive child: Victim and architect of a coercive system. In E. J. Mash, L. A. Hamerlynck, & L. C. Handy (Eds.), *Behavior modification and families*. New York: Brunner/Mazel, 1976. (a)

Patterson, G. R. *Living with children* (Rev. ed.). Champaign, Ill.: Research Press, 1976. (b)

Patterson, G. R., Cobb, J. A., & Ray, R. S. A social engineering technology for retraining the families of aggressive boys. In H. E. Adams & I. P. Unikel (Eds.), *Issues and trends in behavior therapy*. Springfield, Ill.: Charles C Thomas, 1973.

Patterson, G. R., & Fagot, B. I. Selective responsiveness to social reinforcers and deviant behavior in children. *Psychological Record*, 1967, *17*, 369-378.

Patterson, G. R., & Fleischman, M. J. Maintenance of treatment effects: Some considerations concerning family systems and follow-up data. *Behavior Therapy*, 1979, *10*, 168-185.

Patterson, G. R., & Reid, J. B. Intervention for families of aggressive boys: A replication study. *Behaviour Research and Therapy*, 1973, *11*, 383-394.

Patterson, G. R., Reid, J. B., Jones, R. R., & Conger, R. E. *A social learning approach to family intervention*. Eugene, Ore.: Castalia, 1975.

Peed, S., Roberts, M., & Forehand, R. Evaluation of the effectiveness of a standardized parent training program in altering the interaction of mothers and their non-compliant children. *Behavior Modification*, 1977, *1*, 323-350.

Peterson, R. F. Power, programming, and punishment: Could we be overcontrolling our children? In E. J. Mash, L. A. Hamerlynck, & L. C. Handy (Eds.), *Behavior modification and families*. New York: Brunner/Mazel, 1976.

Porter, B., & O'Leary, K. D. Marital discord and childhood behavior problems. *Journal of Abnormal Child Psychology*, 1980, *8*, 287-295.

Rickard, K. M., Forehand, R., Wells, K. C., Griest, D. L., & McMahon, R. J. Factors in the referral of children for behavioral treatment: A comparison of mothers of clinic-referred deviant, clinic-referred nondeviant, and non-clinic children. *Behaviour Research and Therapy*, 1981, *19*, 201-205.

Risley, T. R., Clark, H. B., & Cataldo, M. F. Behavioral technology for the normal middle-class family. In E. J. Mash, L. A. Hamerlynck, & L. C. Handy (Eds.), *Behavior modification and families*. New York: Brunner/Mazel, 1976.

Roberts, M. W., McMahon, R. J., Forehand, R., & Humphreys, L. The effect of parental instruction-giving on child compliance. *Behavior Therapy*, 1978, *9*, 793-798.

Robins, L. N. Follow-up studies. In H. C. Quay & J. S. Werry (Eds.), *Psychopathological disorders of childhood* (2nd ed.). New York: Wiley, 1979.

Rosen, G. M. The development and use of nonprescription behavior therapies. *American Psychologist*, 1976, *31*, 139-141.

Rosen, G. M. Nonprescription behavior therapies and other self-help treatments: A reply to Goldiamond. *American Psychologist*, 1977, *32*, 178-179.

Rudestam, K. E., Fisher, R. H., & Fiester, A. R. Differential effectiveness of mother vs. stranger in the control of children with behavior problems: An experiment in child swapping. *Psychological Reports*, 1974, *35*, 823-833.

Sajwaj, T., & Dillon, A. Complexities of an "elementary" behavior modification procedure: Differential adult attention used for children's behavior disorders. In B. C. Etzel, J. M. LeBlanc, & D. M. Baer (Eds.), *New developments in behavioral research: Theory, method, and application*. Hillsdale, N.J.: Erlbaum, 1977.

Salzinger, K., Feldman, R. S., & Portnoy, S. Training parents of brain-injured children in the use of operant conditioning procedures. *Behavior Therapy*, 1970, *1*, 4-32.

Scarboro, M. E., & Forehand, R. Effects of response-contingent isolation and ignoring on compliance and oppositional behavior of children. *Journal of Experimental Child Psychology*, 1975, *19*, 252-264.

Spielberger, C. D., Gorsuch, R. L., & Lushene, R. E. *STAI manual for the State-Trait Anxiety Inventory*. Palo Alto, Calif.: Consulting Psychologists Press, 1970.

Tavormina, J. B., Henggeler, S. W., & Gayton, W. F. Age trends in parental assessments of behavior problems of their retarded children. *Mental Retardation*, 1976, *14*, 38-39.

Tharp, R. G., & Wetzel, R. J. *Behavior modification in the natural environment*. New York: Academic Press, 1969.

Thomas, A., Chess, S., & Birch, H. G. *Temperament and behavior*. New York: New York University Press, 1968.

Thomas, A., Chess, S., Birch, H. G., Hertzig, M., & Korn, S. *Behavioral individuality in early childhood*. New York: New York University Press, 1963.

Wahl, G., Johnson, S. M., Johansson, S., & Martin, S. An operant analysis of child-family interaction. *Behavior Therapy*, 1974, *5*, 64-78.

Wahler, R. G. Deviant child behavior within the family: Developmental speculations and behavior change strategies. In H. Leitenberg (Ed.), *Handbook of behavior modification and behavior therapy*. Englewood Cliffs, N.J.: Prentice-Hall, 1976.

Wahler, R. G. The insular mother: Her problems in parent-child treatment. *Journal of Applied Behavior Analysis*, 1980, *13*, 207-219.

Wahler, R. G., & Afton, A. D. Attentional processes in insular and noninsular mothers: Some differences in their summary reports about child problem behavior. *Child Behavior Therapy*, 1980, *2*, 25-42.

Weathers, L. R., & Liberman, R. P. Modification of family behavior. In D. Marholin (Ed.), *Child behavior therapy*. New York: Gardner Press, 1977.

Wells, K. C., & Forehand, R. Child behavior problems in the home. In S. M.

Turner, K. Calhoun, & H. E. Adams (Eds.), *Handbook of clinical behavior therapy*. New York: Wiley, 1981.

Wells, K. C., Forehand, R., Griest, D. L. Generality of treatment effects from treated to untreated behaviors resulting from a parent training program. *Journal of Clinical Child Psychology*, 1980, *9*, 217-219.

Wells, K. C., Griest, D. L., & Forehand, R. The use of a self-control package to enhance temporal generality of a parent training program. *Behaviour Research and Therapy*, 1980, *18*, 347-358.

Williams, C. D. The elimination of tantrum behaviors by extinction procedures. *Journal of Abnormal and Social Psychology*, 1959, *59*, 269-270.

Williams, J. G., Barlow, D. H., & Agras, W. S. Behavioral measurement of severe depression. *Archives of General Psychiatry*, 1972, *27*, 330-333.

Wiltz, N. A., & Patterson, G. R. An evaluation of parent training procedures designed to alter inappropriate aggressive behavior of boys. *Behavior Therapy*, 1974, *5*, 215-221.

Wittes, G., & Radin, N. *Parent manual on child rearing*. Unpublished manuscript, 1968. (Available from Ypsilanti Early Education Program, Ypsilanti, Michigan.)

Wolf, M. M. Social validity: The case for subjective measurement or how applied behavior analysis is finding its heart. *Journal of Applied Behavior Analysis*, 1978, *11*, 203-214.

Worland, J., Carney, R. M., Weinberg, H., & Milich, R. Dropping out of group behavioral parent training. *Behavioral Counseling Quarterly*, in press.

AUTHOR AND SUBJECT INDEXES

AUTHOR INDEX

SUBJECT INDEX